KIMBERLY

HOPE FOR THE SOUL

Make Yourself at Home in God's Heart

©2017 by Kimberly Michelle Ford All rights reserved. No part of this book may be reproduced in any form without permission in writing from the author, except in the case of brief quotations embodied in critical articles or reviews.

All Scripture quotations, unless otherwise indicated, are taken from the Holy Bible, New International Version®, NIV®. Copyright © 1973, 1978,1984, 2011 by Biblica, Inc.™ Used by permission of Zondervan. All rights reserved worldwide. www.zondervan.com. The "NIV" and "New International Version" are trademarks registered in the United States Patent and Trademark Office by Biblica, Inc. ™

Scripture quotations marked NKJV are taken from the New King James Version. Copyright© 1982, 1992 by Thomas Nelson, Inc. Used by permission All rights reserved.

Scripture quotations marked "The MSG Bible" are taken from The Message Bible. Copyright © 1993, 1994, 1995, 1996, 2000, 2001, 2002. Used by permission of NavPress Publishing Group.

Interior Design by: https://www.fiverr.com/darkcoderx Muhammad Asif
Cover Design by: https://www.fiverr.com/Jesh Jesh Designs
Cover Photo: Orpheus and Aphrodite Photography, LLC.

Library of Congress Control Number: 2017912193
CreateSpace Independent Publishing Platform, North Charleston, SC

ISBN-13: 978-1548661007 (CreateSpace-Assigned)
ISBN-10: 1548661007
BISAC: Religion / Christian Life / Spiritual Growth

*This book is written and dedicated to my children—
Tramayne, Jessika, and Jordan*

•

Don't lose your grip on Love and Loyalty.
Tie them around your neck; carve their initials on your heart.
Earn a reputation for living well
in God's eyes and the eyes of the people.

Proverbs 3:3-4 MSG

CONTENTS

ACKNOWLEDGEMENT i
FOREWORD iii
INTRODUCTION: Make Yourself At Home in God's Heart v
CHAPTER 1: GETTING UP: AFTER THE FALL 1
CHAPTER 2: EVERY CRISIS IS AN OPPORTUNITY 13
CHAPTER 3: ARE YOU STANDING? 19
CHAPTER 4: MATTERS OF THE HEART 25
CHAPTER 5: PREVAIL AND EXCEL 33
CHAPTER 6: JESUS SAVED US ALL 43
CHAPTER 7: CONFIDENCE TO PRESS FORWARD 51
CHAPTER 8: HIS WORKMANSHIP & AN EXPENSIVE GUARANTEE ... 59
CHAPTER 9: OUR FAITH—HIS WILL 67
CHAPTER 10: BUT WHAT I DO HAVE, I GIVE IT 75
CHAPTER 11: RIGHT NOW—I AM 83
CHAPTER 12: FINDING YOUR PLACE, WHILE IN THE PROCESS ... 91
CHAPTER 13: YOUR TIME IS NOW 99
CHAPTER 14: DON'T STOP HERE–KEEP GOING—FINISH THE RACE .. 107
CHAPTER 15: YOU'VE ALREADY WON THE BATTLE 111
CHAPTER 16: THE ENEMY, THE SOUL, & THE PROMISE OF HOPE ... 117

CHAPTER 17: A Message to Challenge You 123
CHAPTER 18 From Windows To Doors 131
CHAPTER 19: Take It All Back…and Then Some 137
CHAPTER 20: A Shield of Favor 145
CHAPTER 21: Deliver Me from Disappointment 153

FINAL REFLECTION: Paid in Full 163
REFERENCES 164
ABOUT THE AUTHOR 167

Acknowledgement

Apostle Long,

You have impacted my life in so many indescribable ways. It was truly an honor to be chosen to travel to the homeless outreach centers each month and deliver messages of hope and salvation to the homeless community. It is because I walked with you in spirit, that I learned how to minister by your example. I came to know your heart for people. As you pushed me to arise from my own turmoil and disappointments, I pushed them. You taught me in your life's example how to love the lost and the unlovable. You also taught me that no matter what situation we in humanity find ourselves in, we are all deserving of an abundant and high-quality life. You taught me that no matter what pit we may fall into, we all deserve to be treated as the royalty we are. You taught me to raise my expectation of God as well as my standard of living. Hence, I have been ignited to teach others the same. It was always my goal to make sure that we showed up at the shelter ready to serve with excellence and with love, because they deserved our best.

The day we laid you to rest, I stood by your casket comforting our grieving brothers and sisters who would come to say their farewell. This would be the last time I would get to stand for you, honor you, and lift up your arms. I repeatedly heard your voice in the spirit, *"Tell, them I love them."* So for each grieving heart I did just that. Some looked in amazement that your love for us still speaks. Some hugged me and thanked me. But at that moment, you amazed even me. Your love for our church family and humanity at large exceeds that of most. Sometimes, I even wonder did we deserve you. Your sacrifice goes beyond what most of us could possibly endure. As a Spiritual Father to so many of us, your example taught us how to bend and not break, stand and not fight, love and not hate.

"Thank you" just won't do.
Therefore, I am eternally grateful.
I love you *Pops*!

Rest in Heaven
5.12.1953—1.15.2017

Foreword

HOPE. What is it? Where is it? In a "less" world, we have to remember that we serve a God of more than enough. All throughout our daily walk, we see the hopeless, the helpless, the homeless, the heartless… and if we allow ourselves to be consumed by what we see, it will eventually become who we are. It's easy to allow the burdens of society to reduce us to the expectations of the finite minds of those around us. No doubt, it is one of Satan's greatest joys to see us without hope. The Bible forewarns us that the devil is like a roaring lion, seeking whom he may devour. We see the evidence of it each and every day. Pandemonium has become commonplace, and peace is foreign land. In today's culture, even the children of God seem to have come to expect and embrace the darkness.

HOPE. While it seems evasive, we should take courage in the knowledge that it's not. Hope is within everyone's reach. Most have just been looking in the wrong places. True hope is more than optimism and anticipation. It can't be found in material things. It can't be found in fallible man. Hope—the unfailing, flawless kind—can only be found in Christ Jesus. And until we look to Him, it will always elude us.

In *Hope for the Soul*, author Kimberly Ford uses relatable and personal examples to show the length and depth of God's grace and mercy. Combining real world instances and the Word of God, she proves beyond a shadow of a doubt that the King (our Lord and Savior) trumps any card that the enemy may try to deal in this proverbial game called life.

HOPE. Find it here—between the pages of this thought-provoking book.

~ Kendra Norman (National bestselling author of "I Shall Not Die" and "The Path from Pain to Purpose")

Make Yourself At Home in God's Heart

I pray this book touches the hearts of each and every reader. No matter who you are or what you have experienced in life—I am convinced that each of us have had an experience with rejection, abandonment, and/or inadequacy. Like many of you, I am familiar with the effects of family dysfunction and its ability to create long term relational dysfunction. No matter how much we try to pretend and portray the "picture perfect" family, it just does not exist. Hollywood writers haven't even succeeded at creating a perfect television family.

For a huge portion of my life, I have struggled to combat a sense of physical and emotional displacement. When we experience abuse, abandonment, and rejection as children we grow up with all sorts of self-sabotaging behaviors. My self-sabotaging behavior, for many years, has been allowing abusive people to come into my life and control my self-perception. This is mostly due to the abuse I witnessed and the sexual abuse I endured as a child. As a result, I developed into a woman who subconsciously believed that this abuse was normal. I subsequently believed I deserved it. Sadly, I grew to believe that this was love. I did not develop a healthy set of boundaries as a child. So over the years, when I have been mistreated by the people close to me, I was quick to forgive their behavior out of fear of losing the relationship. Unfortunately, I had unconsciously subscribed to the idea that this was the best God had to offer me. I didn't realize I deserved better, so I expected and settled for less from people.

But after more than 30 years of harboring a negative self-image, I started serving God's people. I began giving back to the homeless and there I was re-introduced to God. I discovered that I was not alone in my pain. Though I had a home and a place to lay my head at night, I recognized a familiar characteristic in the hearts of the homeless. God revealed to me in an instant the pain in their hearts. Amazingly, their pain matched my pain. Most of the homeless men and women I mentored and served, carried the same pain of rejection and abandonment. And in serving them, there arrived a sense of inclusion for me. It feels good to connect with someone who "just knows" exactly how you feel without asking you to explain.

Like them, I understood how it felt to be outcast or viewed as less valuable by the people closest to you. So I gave them what I knew they so desperately longed for: genuine embrace and love—without judgement, terms, or conditions. As I witnessed some of the other volunteers cringe or turn their noses at the thought of coming in close contact with them, I gladly reached out to release all the love God wanted to shower on them. Many of them were surprised at my excitement and eagerness to hug or touch them.

During this particular season in my life, God taught me how to love people—in conjunction with the way He loved me. It doesn't matter who has hurt me, left me or verbally torn me down, I can always come home to Him and expect to be comforted. He taught me that home doesn't just shelter us from the rain. But it's also the place where we can release the tears. It's where we can receive authentic, unconditional, and unlimited love. It's where the broken places in us are gently mended back together again. Home is where the walls of confidence that have been demolished down to rubble, will be rebuilt stronger than before.

The little girl in me, who struggled to find acceptance and inclusion in the world, discovered that the only place this type of fortifying love exists is in God's heart. As a result, I found the courage to walk away from unhealthy relationships, correct destructive thought patterns, and pursue my dreams with confidence. I also found the power that comes from seeking only God to fulfill my desire for love.

When you make yourself at home in God's heart, prepare to have your life shifted with a renewed perspective on how you love yourself and others. Only those who are fulfilled by His love can open up their hearts to forgive their enemies and release them from every offense. In this book *"Hope For the Soul"*, I pray you learn that you can take every issue you face home to God. Being the loving Father that He is, He will meet you at the door excited with open arms and ready to receive you. The healing, the love, and the acceptance you need will only be found *in His heart*.

~Kimberly Michelle Ford

Trust GOD from the bottom of your heart;
don't try to figure out everything on your own.
Listen for GOD's voice in everything you do, everywhere you go;
He's the one who will keep you on track.
Don't assume that you know it all.
Run to GOD! Run from evil!
Your body will glow with health,
your very bones will vibrate with life!
Honor GOD with everything you own;
give Him the first and the best.
Your barns will burst,
your wine vats will brim over.
But don't, dear friend, resent GOD's discipline;
don't sulk under His loving correction.
It's the child He loves that GOD corrects;
a Father's delight is behind all this.

Proverbs 3:5-12 The MSG Bible

1

Getting up: After the Fall

How many of you know what it's like to fall? And I don't mean trip over the curb and scrape your knee or stomp your toe. But I am referring to a fall from a high place—all the way down to an extremely low place. I mean like falling down a flight of, what may appear to be, a never-ending staircase to utterly fall *flat on your face*. No matter how you braced yourself, all of your attempts to slow the progression of your fall *would fail*. Upon landing, every part of your body, soul, and spirit would feel the pain and impact of your crash.

Regardless of our diverse beginnings, whether humble or wealthy, most of us are created with this internal need and desire to accomplish goals that are seemingly impossible. The ambition is woven into the fabric of our being to challenge our limitations, defy the odds against us, and accomplish something that may or may not have been by accomplished by anyone else. We dream dreams that no-one else has dreamed of. We set out to charter courses that no other person has chartered before. We seek to build businesses that offer a product or a service that has never been thought of. Or we simply seek to advance technology in order to offer society a faster or more effective way of existing. Since the beginning of time, we have worked extremely hard to excel at something greater than our assumed capacity. We all want to leave a mark in this world, to have our name remembered, to have our existence count for something—other than simply existing. We all want to be *GREAT!!*

While we are on our course to being great—the higher we climb and the closer we get to our dreams becoming reality—we grow *confident* that our goals are on track. We are confident that we are indeed a genius and our blueprint for success will work after all. We may have a few delays and setbacks along the way. But as we keep climbing we grow even more *confident*. But then the unexpected crash occurs. We hit a wall, and our efforts appear to have all been in vain. It now appears that all of our work was wrong, our hopes were misdirected and it appears that instead of going up we have been on this kamikaze downward spiral crash all along! Stricken with disappointment and grief, we realize that we cannot go any further in the direction we were headed. We must now find the dignity, the courage, *and the will* to dream a new dream.

> For a righteous man falls seven times, and rises again...
>
> Proverbs 24:16 AMP

The Bible gives us countless examples in regards to falling. We are promised that even after falling from a place of security and confidence we have the strength to rise again—with greater insights, greater strength, and greater wisdom. If you are reading this book, it is my guess that you can relate to having fallen before and may possibly need the encouragement to rise again. It is my prayer that you find that here!

For many years I have been honored to mentor and speak at homeless shelters. Never once, have I taken these opportunities to share from my own personal experiences for granted. It is an honor to share with others who needed the encouragement to keep fighting even when it appears that defeat is certain. To be quite honest, it was truly humbling to show up at the shelters each month and see a room filled with people interested enough to sit and listen to the stories about my personal issues and how I overcame them. As the years went by my amazement grew as they continued to show up.

Many of them walked or rode the bus a very long distance. In the heat of the summer and on the most frigid winter days, some rolled in their wheelchairs across town each month. Most of the people I mentored were suffering from physical and mental infirmities for a very long time. Countless veterans were there each month to seek the love and embrace of someone else who understood their struggles of being rejected by the same society they had given their lives to protect. Most of their families and friends had written them off and classified them as crazy, weird, or just unreachable. After fighting to not allow this life to be the result of their efforts, they had given in to the notion of failure. Life has been a constant uphill climb and their souls were tired. They had now embraced the idea that the life they would live existed in the streets, under bridges, and in parks and shelters. In summary, each of the people God blessed me to inspire lacked the adequate resources for survival and had not been happy or even breathed a sigh of relief in quite some time. So each month when I checked in at the shelter, it was my goal to allow that to happen, I wanted them to breathe a sigh of relief even if only for a few hours.

> Though I am free and belong to no one, I have made myself a slave to everyone, to win as many as possible.
>
> 1 Corinthians 9:19-23 NIV

Unlike our materialistic society that would prefer to turn a blind eye to the less fortunate and poor in spirit, I simply could not take their lives for granted. Like them I had experienced multiple "great falls" in my own life. I knew, like they knew, what it feels like to constantly be on an upward climb, yet never feel relieved from the pressures of life. I felt that since God had chosen and equipped me with the capacity to keep going, I realized that I owed them something. I owed them my testimony, my hand, and my heart.

In 2011, I suffered a great fall. My life had drastically changed since my divorce and I was working very hard to build a secure foundation to support my children. I found my passion for helping people through my work in the employment industry. So I was determined to build a career in the field. For well over a year, I had worked to position myself for a new role; a role that would allow me to use the untapped potential that lay dormant inside me.

Getting up: After the Fall

I thought, "*Finally, I will get to play an important role within my company and the glass ceiling that has held me back is about to break.*" Over the years, I had been praised for my organizational talent, leadership, and professionalism. But the promotions I sought after would never go through. Then when it finally did, the recession of 2008 began and the owner of the business closed his doors, just 6 weeks after I started my new leadership role. This time I felt it would be different. It's 2011 and after a life of glass ceilings and closed doors, I have managed to hope again for the opportunity to be a successful business leader. I had waited and served my organization for 2 years now. For 10 years, I had even endured the pain of watching others younger, quicker, and more charismatic be promoted much sooner than me. But surely because of my resilient faith and endurance, *it's my time right?*

Well the day finally came and I woke up with the great expectation of hearing the great news outlining the details of my promotion. But as I started out the door, dressed to impress, I tell the kids, "Wake up and get your day started, I love you, I am leaving now." I started down the stairs. The first step went well. But after the 2nd step, something unexpected occurred. My left foot went forward to take the 3rd step and my right foot didn't follow. The heel of my shoe had gotten caught in the carpet and the hem of my jeans stayed there to watch. It was a fearful ride down the remaining flight of stairs; desperately grabbing at spindles and rails to help stop the wreck. And I painfully landed face 1st-fingers 2nd onto the carpet at the bottom of the staircase.

For a few moments, I lay there entertaining the idea of calling it a day. I envisioned myself lying there and then phoning my boss to inform her of my calamity. I envisioned myself back in bed. Then, I remembered…today is "*the day*". No way would I waste all those days of waiting for an answer by giving in to a fall down the stairs. Somehow, at that moment, the fall down the stairs became irrelevant, and the pain I felt unimportant. So I mustered up a shout for help, which by the way confirmed my daughters fear, and she came running down screaming, traumatized herself at the sight of her mother lying at the foot of the stairs. She reached out, grabbed my hand and helped me to roll over onto my feet. I grabbed my purse and straightened out my wrinkles, then started out the door.

I got to work just in time. I limped off the elevator, down the hallway and made it to my desk. Focused on the assurance of victory, I started my day. I'm cross-training new hires for the job they are about to begin, when an email alert pops up on the screen. It reads, "I am considering you for my open position effective February 1st (which was literally 1 week away), could you please send me your information which confirms you have met or exceeded your 4th Quarter goals?" Well I knew I had met them so I was equally excited to respond.

After lunch, my boss makes it into the office and about an hour or two later, she comes over with a blank look and says can you come by my office. "It's time! She's got good news, I can just feel it!" So I stand up and carefully walk towards her office and I take a seat smiling. She has trouble starting, but nevertheless she starts.

We were measured by a performance pyramid for the last two quarters in the previous year. However, the executive leadership had discovered that the performance metrics we were measured by were flawed and in fact a set up for failure. Several people were negatively affected by the measurements so the management team discontinued use of the performance plan and changed the way they measured our performance—starting January 1st. My boss was here to tell me that unfortunately for me, the performance pyramid still had enough time to do one more injustice...*to me!*

The leader's refused to promote me on the basis of the pyramid, though it was proven to be a flawed measurement. And like the fall down the stairs earlier that morning, I only wanted to belt out a scream for help! Symbolically, as my body plunged towards the bottom of the staircase, my dream of advancing up this corporate ladder reaching for success took its own plunge towards the ground. I couldn't respond verbally without breaking down in my bosses' office.

I finally made it home after a long ride screaming in tears. I spent the night crying in my sleep as I switched back and forth between "It's not fair", "How could this happen again?", "I've worked so hard", and "I'm just tired of it all". Twice in the same day I had felt the impact of a crash landing and they both left me in an enormous amount of pain. But my season of falling would not end so soon.

Exactly one week after the day of disaster, I recognized a pain in my stomach that never would seem to subside. At first I thought, "it's the stress in my life: work, kids, school, and ministry". Then I thought "It's only my nerves, I'm just nervous and excited about this promotion". Then after the promotion failed, the following week, I began to question "Why is my stomach still in painful knots?" By Friday, I was experiencing a pain that just would not go away. By 4 o'clock, I determined that I must go straight to the emergency room after work.

I finally arrived at the emergency room at 8:00pm. Just my luck: the emergency room is packed to capacity! All the beds are full and its standing room only. Here I am in pain, like many others, and the place of my healing is overflowed with the sick. After several hours of waiting in pain, it was my turn. I lay there on the table as the nurse performed an ultrasound. The doctor came in at around 3:30 am and lays it on me, "Your gallbladder is packed with stones, and you must have surgery immediately." I sat there amazed and confused all at once. How could this have happened to me? This issue doesn't run in my family; why am I here? There must be some mistake!

The doctor assured me he was correct and that I was being admitted to the hospital and prepared for surgery. What an unexpected and inconvenient blow to my life. I thought first about how to get my kids situated. But my second immediate thought would be, "Will it be quick, I have to be at work Monday morning?" My aunt asked the doctor, "How long will the recovery process be?" He responds, "7-10 days". I am now thinking, "Oh my Lord! How in the world will I be a mother to three kids, continue my classes, and go to work if I am on bed rest for 7-10 days?" It sounded like such a long time. But God had a plan!

My surgery went well the next day and by night time I was being rushed out of there to go home to rest and recover. But in less than 1 week other complications arose, my stitches had burst and I found myself back in the hospital again. The doctor was forced to send me back in to surgery for repair.

As crazy as it sounds: after the 2nd surgery I took another fall down the stairs! To top things all off, one week later I discovered that due to all of the time off work, I would not receive full payment from work and as a result would not be able to pay my basic bills. I could not begin to fathom what in the world God was doing.

Many times God will call us to a place of disaster; tear our lives apart, all so that He can begin to put us back together again. It was truly not my desire to be thrown down a flight of stairs twice, fail at a much sought after job promotion, and then slammed across a surgery table—twice in 7 days. It was obvious that God was speaking loud and clear in my life and He wanted to get my attention. The way we may expect for our lives to be elevated, quite normally, never go according to our plans. But what I began to learn is that God can do whatever He wants to do, however He wants to do it, and I have *no say-so* in the matter.

> But He knows the way that I take: when He has tested me I shall come forth as gold.
>
> **Job 23:10 NKJV**

In the beginning of this entire calamity, I would have rested on the idea that my balance, my harvest, my health, and my finances were all under an attack of the enemy. Over the years, I have learned that it is very important to seek God and hear from Him when we are in complex situations. Many times we may see things one way, but something else contrary to our logic may very well be taking place. I would be remiss if I did not honor Him by saying "It was He that ultimately tested *my strength, my heart, my will and my faith.*" Though I entered that year with high hopes and great expectations for this new season of my life, I soon discovered it would not be an easy walk in the park.

Many of us have sought God for direction, and then devised strategic plans to be successful. We have even submitted them to God in prayer and believed in His word for the blessing. However, the enemy is *never* far away. He is always watching, listening, and waiting for the opportunity to destroy the harvest. Jesus informed us that He came that we might have life and have it more *abundantly*. But he also carefully reminded us that the enemy comes in quickly; "like a thief, to steal, kill, and destroy".

After the first fall down the stairs I questioned God, "Why did I fall? Why am I here? And it hurt so bad that I even asked myself, "Do I even want to get up?" And even though I had all these questions, in my mind I pictured my promotion coming that day. So I could not stay there! At the bottom of the stairs, I created a picture in my mind of me in a better place. So that gave me the strength to get back up again. Only I got to work to find out that even though I pressed past my place of pain, I would get no promotion. I had taken the time to properly plan, I networked for the promotion, I excelled at presentations, and I served and performed at a level of excellence. After my recovery from surgery, I went back to work and found out that they had also given my next promotion away (the one I would have been considered for as a backup). I went in the bathroom stall and I cried like a 5-year old who had lost her way home. Now, it truly seemed that all of my efforts had gone down in vain!

I began to wonder, "Why God, Why now?" I wondered, "God, Why me? I'm yours, I serve you and I'm working to help your people, my motives are pure. But I am watching as all my enemies are prospering. Where is my reward!!??" I am willing to admit I was angry and I thought I deserved more. I felt I deserved immediate answers. For a brief moment in my life, I forgot that He is God all by Himself. I did not know God's plan and He would surely not reveal it to me as I approached Him in such anger.

All I knew was, I wanted to be a leader and I also needed the extra money to provide for my children. I was tired of being in a position less than my capacity to perform. How many of you have said, "I'm better than this! I'm better than poverty! I'm better than this wheelchair! I'm better than government assistance! I'm better than handouts!" I asked God, "Where is Your glory in all of this??? How can you possibly be getting the glory in my pain? You are supposed to get the victory. Your people are supposed to prosper. So what in the world is going on God???"

When I came out of the bathroom as I began to walk back to my desk, He responded to my cries for an answer so clearly, "You said I could use you right?" Like a child caught in her foolishness, I could only reply, "Huh?" Then I heard His voice again, "YOU SAID I COULD USE YOU RIGHT??" Right then and there, I learned a powerful, yet painful, lesson. Many times we ask God to use us, but we never expect for it to hurt. We never expect to lose jobs, things, or people dear to us. We never expect for Him to change our plans. We don't expect to be disappointed. We never expect for Him to remove us from our place of comfort or security. I have learned that by surrendering to God, you are subjecting yourself to His ultimate plan for your life. If you sincerely ask God to use you, He will surely answer your prayer. But be prepared for Him to use you in His own way. *He is GOD! And He can use you how He chooses!!! He is not concerned with our feelings.*

> Thus says God the Lord, "Behold the former things have come to pass, and new things I declare; Before they spring forth I tell you of them."
>
> Isaiah 42:9 NKJV

I began to reflect on the relationships that I had been praying for; several of which I had been praying for years. I realized my closest friend of over 20 years and I were no longer fighting. My boss, who was agnostic, told me over lunch with tears rolling down her face, that she was truly "blessed" by having known me. She even contributed $200 into the payment for my monthly bills. My director who was on the fence with his relationship with God, often joked about the biblical principles I lived by and my submission to my spiritual father. But during my darkest season, God touched his heart and he also blessed me financially to cover bills after my surgery. My sister, whom had always lived a troubled life, and was on and off homeless for the past 10 years, called me the day after I lost the 1st promotion. I will never forget the sound of her voice, "Kim, I got my own apartment!!" Instantly, after reflecting on God's work happening around me, I began to see the breaking of day. I began to understand the purpose for my storm, and then it didn't hurt quite as much. I began to see the light. I began to realize that everybody around me was observing how I managed this dark season in my life. And as I kept going, when others would have quit, they were recognizing why I was able to stand. As a result, they too were being empowered and God was indeed getting the glory—in my storm.

Once I realized that my fall had a purpose (and that I wasn't just being tossed and driven by the wind with no course in mind) then I could accept His perfect will for my life. I don't know about you, but I need for my storm to make sense. I don't have time to go through a storm—*just to be going through it!* People say God will do things that don't make sense. But I am here to tell you, even though God's ways are not our ways, nor His thought our thoughts, *He will indeed reveal His secret wisdom to His people.*

It may not always be what you want to hear, it may not be a plan that's comfortable to you....But *He will* reveal His plans to you. And as long as you let God help you make sense of your fall, then you can trust Him to bring you through it! God will not just bring you to the test. But He will bring you *through it*! After this, I began to realize the purpose of a fall: *Sometimes you have to come to the end of yourself in order for God to step in and do the miraculous in your life.*

So let's talk about getting up after the fall. Earlier, I said God tested my *strength*. After feeling like I had fallen one too many times, I was sort of shell-shocked. My body was weak and numb. I said,

- ❖ "God I can't take it anymore!"
- ❖ "I don't have the strength to go through another disappointment".
- ❖ "I don't have the strength to go through another sickness".
- ❖ "I don't have the strength to stand on the ROCK anymore".
- ❖ "I am tired!"

But Paul reminded me in 2 Corinthians 12:9, *"God's grace is sufficient for thee: for my strength is made perfect in weakness. Most gladly therefore will I rather glory in my infirmities, that the power of Christ may rest upon me."* It is when I have fallen and have nothing left in me to get up, that the power of Christ lifted me back to my feet!! For it is when we are weak that HE is STRONG!!

I told you earlier that God tried and tested *my faith.* Hebrew 11:6 tells us *'But without faith it is impossible to please Him: for He that cometh to God must believe that He is, and that He is a rewarder of them that diligently seek Him".* After several attempts to seek a promotion on my job I finally said, "I give up, maybe this is all God has for me, I said like the widow woman that was ready to bake a cake and die, "I guess I will take this little that I have and die."

But God says in Hebrews 10:23 *Let us hold fast the profession of our faith without wavering; For He who has promised is faithful!!* That means I had to make a decision. After several days and weeks of saying, "I give up!" I had to change my thoughts. I had to renew my mind. I had to change my perception of God's work in my life. Romans 12:2 says: *And be not conformed to this world: but be ye transformed by the renewing of your mind, that ye may prove what is that good, and acceptable, and perfect, will of God.*

God's plan was not to destroy me, it was to prosper me. I had interviewed with another company and they were very interested in me. I told a close friend about it and in her excitement she said, "Girl I'm claiming that job for you!" I told her, "No don't claim anything! I don't want to be disappointed". Just that quick, the enemy had locked my mind up in fear and the expectation of failure. That quick, in my subconscious, I had decided that God's word just might not be true. But Satan is a liar and the father of all lies. Every seed he sows is a lie. Every work he produces is a lie.

> The natural person does not accept the things of the Spirit of God, for they are folly to him, and he is not able to understand them because they are spiritually discerned.
>
> **1 Corinthians 2:14**

So, I started the next morning by declaring, "I do believe his Word". Then the next day it was "I am the head and not the tail! I am seated above and never beneath, I am a lender not a borrower, I am blessed coming in and blessed going out!" The next day my declaration was "Kim you are more than a conqueror and you can do ALL things through Him… not some…but ALL!"

Here is how He tested *my heart*. Job 13:15 says: *Though He slay me, yet will I trust in Him*. I love God with all my heart, my mind, and soul. *But He tested even that—my LOVE for Him!* I had to trust that my love relationship with God would see me through any adversity I would ever face.

In order to get up from the falls, I had to make a conscious decision to *trust Him* with my life. *I had to learn how to trust Him with my fall.* If God calls you to a low place, there is nothing you can do to stop it! It's like falling down the stairs; as you see yourself drawing closer to the bottom, you reach for the rails and you try to stop the descension. But once the fall is in motion, *there is no turning back!*

I had to learn that, as I saw another fall coming, I would need to brace myself for the fall and trust Him to meet me there. I had to trust that God had a plan and a purpose for my fall. I had to trust, like Job, that even though God allowed the fall, He already had a plan to restore my life with double for my trouble. I had to trust that God had a plan to prosper me, a plan to keep me in good health, and a plan to prosper my soul! I had to trust in the Lord with all my heart and lean not to my own understanding. I had to trust that He would direct my path!!!

Getting up is never easy. But you have to know beyond the shadow of a doubt—that it's not over until God says it's over! This is not the end… and tomorrow's joy will be much greater than yesterday's pain. The very minute you change your way of thinking, *anything* could happen. It's not over for you!

God has a plan to move you from yesterday's fall to tomorrows rise to glory. No matter how bad it looks, nothing is impossible for God. Everything you need has already been provided for you. But you have got to believe. You have got to get past the disappointment, get past the pain, and move towards His grace. God has given you the grace to *get up!!*

2

Every Crisis Is An Opportunity

Humanity is not lacking in its list of unanswered questions for God. Our unanswered questions flood our thoughts both consciously and subconsciously. Until our minds are satisfied with some sort of resolve or understanding, we will resist letting go of the desire to have the origin our existence explained. When we wake up in the morning they start circling in our minds:

- ❖ Who am I?
- ❖ What is my purpose?
- ❖ Why did I have to go through what I went through?
- ❖ How did I get here?
- ❖ How do I get back?
- ❖ Why didn't God intervene?

And as you lie down at night your mind is still asking:
- ❖ Where do I go from here?
- ❖ How do I start again?
- ❖ How do I love again?
- ❖ How do I trust again?
- ❖ Where will I end up?

Paul addresses the church at Corinth:

"Because of this decision we don't evaluate people by what they have or how they look. We looked at the Messiah that way once and got it all wrong, as you know. We certainly don't look at him that way anymore. Now we look inside, and what we see is that anyone united with the Messiah gets a fresh start, is created new. The old life is gone; a new life burgeons! Look at it! All this comes from the God who settled the relationship between us and him, and then called us to settle our relationships with each other. God put the world square with himself through the Messiah, giving the world a fresh start by offering forgiveness of sins."

2 Corinthians 5:17 The MSG Bible

Most of us have fought as we struggled to transition from an old way of living, an old relationship, or an old state of being—into the new creature God intended for you to be. There is a 3-phase cycle we must all encounter in order to get from *here* to *there*, wherever *there is* for you. This cycle resembles the process of the butterfly; larva, cocoon, then emerging of the butterfly. The caterpillar *separates* himself as he crawls into the cocoon. Then it remains in the cocoon for a period to grow and *transform* from one life-form to another. And then at an appointed time, what was once a small caterpillar has been promoted to spread its wings and *emerge* as a butterfly.

The children of Israel experienced their *separation* as they left Egypt, endured their *transformation* in the wilderness for 40 years, and then *emerged* as their descendants entered the Promised Land. When Jonah refused to follow the will of God, he went through his *separation* as he jumped off the boat during the storm, his *transformation* while trapped in the belly of a whale, and then his *emergence* as the whale spit him out and caused him to land right where God initially intended for him to be.

Both of these examples resemble the process of Jesus' crucifixion at the cross: there was a death, a burial, and a resurrection. Forced by the Roman government and betrayed by the Jews, Jesus was separated from humanity by being led to a painful and bloody crucifixion. Then as he showed up in hell right at Satan's doorstep to claim the keys to the kingdom he was transformed into Jesus "THE CHRIST". And on the 3rd day He emerged from the grave with all power in his hands! So like Christ, we must also go through these 3 phases in our quest to discovering our purpose: Separation, Transformation, and Emergence. Let's break down each of the three phases.

In separation, we all go through a process of being stripped away from our comfort zones. Normally, we begin to notice that something doesn't quite feel normal anymore. The things you used to do don't satisfy you anymore. The friends you used to hang out with don't bring you joy anymore. Or sometimes one particular catastrophic event will simply push you from one extreme to the next.

Here is where you have had it up to your ears with confusion and drama. Here is where we have grown tired of one way of life and are kicking and screaming as we are forced into the next phase or dimension of our existence. Simply put, here is where we grow up!

Regardless of which way it happens, you are left feeling alone and isolated from everything and everyone around you. You can be amongst hundreds of people, or either lying in bed next to your spouse, yet still feel like you are there all by yourself.

- ❖ *As the caterpillar is prepared* to begin the process to become a butterfly first it sheds its skin, it becomes naked!! Then it becomes paralyzed, it can't move, no matter what wind comes its way it won't move. But it can at least use its abdominal area to move and make sounds to scare off predators. *And then it enters the cocoon for transformation.*
- ❖ *As the children of Israel* were leaving Egypt, they of course were being chased by Pharaoh's army; they trusted *God* to walk through the Red Sea. They rejoiced all the way through to the other side. Then after the celebration they realized, "We have no food! Moses why did you bring us out here to die? Why are we here? We should have stayed in Egypt!" *Then they entered the wilderness for transformation.*
- ❖ *As Jonah lay in the bottom of the boat*, he heard the crew in chaos above. He remembered the voice of the Lord telling him to "Go to Nineveh". He realized that his disobedience to God's command could cost innocent people their lives. As a leader, he knew he had to get off the boat (and in alignment with God) in order for the storm to cease. So he did just that, and landed in the belly of a whale. *Here is where Jonah entered his place of transformation*

Now in the *transformation phase*, you really get to find out two things: *who God is* and *who you are in Him*. You may easily liken your phase of transformation to that of being tested in the fire. Now that you are by yourself, painful as it may be, you are forced to face the truth. You have obviously exhausted all your resources. All of your clever plans for success have failed you, and you have no more answers! You are bankrupt on ideas. Your body is tired and you have totally surrendered to God. Here is where the silence begins. And here is where God begins to speak life into you. Here is where you have nothing else to depend on but the guiding of the Holy Spirit. It is during transformation that the Holy Spirit is actually able to have its perfect work *in you*.

The butterfly is transforming by spinning silk for her beautiful wings. All the while the butterfly has no idea what her wings will look like. Nevertheless, she will continue to work! She has lost her skin and she's been exposed to the world. She has had to fight off predators, or as we call them haters, naysayers, or abusers. But she knows she has to keep going.

The children of Israel stayed in their wilderness being transformed for 40 years. They realized they had come too far to turn back. They relied on the Lord every day for fresh manna to fall from the sky. Their shoes never wore out, and their clothes were never worn out. They might not have had a lot, but God was transforming them to become a royal nation.

Though Jonah found himself in the bottom of a whale, he knew there was no way out. He was in a mess nobody could save him from but the Lord. I am convinced that Jonah was not in the whale saying, "Oh I'll be out soon, I'll wait it out". Jonah had come to a grim conclusion that he *was not* coming out, "But since I am not coming out, I may as well praise and worship Him while I am here!" And in His worship he was being transformed!

Now here, in *emergence*, is where you get to see God show off through you! Here is when the naysayers get to clasp their mouths in disbelief. How did she get that job? How did he launch such a successful business? How did their marriage survive the cheating? Here is where you have come through the fire, God has restored you to fullness and now people will see the golden radiance of His presence in your life. Now, God gets the glory and you are reaping the rewards.

In emergence you are able to spread your wings and fly; soaring over all those who have doubted you, discredited you, left you, cheated you, lied about you, murdered your dreams, and left you for dead. God gets the glory when you can look at the world and say, "If it had not been for the Lord I would not be here today. Because of His love for me I am still here. Because of His favor I went from the back of the class to the front of the class. Because of His grace I am flying and not dying!!"

We each want to live a peaceful and comfortable life. We each want to experience as least pain as possible. If anyone mentions the word *crisis* or any word associated with it—we automatically go to this disposition of gloom and doom. Crisis will always have a negative stigma assigned to it. In my own journey, I have found myself in crises more often than I would have liked. But I have discovered that what I considered to be a crisis at the time, actually turned out to be the moments that catapulted me to my greatest success.

I am challenging you right now. Begin to look at your issues and ask God, "What do you want me to do differently? What are you trying to show the world, my church, my family, or my community—through me? You will then begin to see your crisis as not merely a moment of personal defeat or desperation. But you will begin to notice that your crisis is really an opportunity for God to teach us all something new. It's an opportunity for all of us to see Him in a different light.

When we emerge from the ashes of our places of defeat we are ultimately saying to the world that we are made of something undeniably great! And everybody, simply everybody wants to have access to that greatness. The greatness that resides in each of us is unique. My greatness cannot be used to conquer your battles, only the battle assigned to me. And it works both ways. The power God placed on the inside of you is strictly and uniquely designed for *your* storms. But to others, we grant access to the power source by going through our own transformation with resilience and then emerging with a testimony for all to see!

3

Are You Standing?

In the days preceding the crucifixion of Jesus Christ, he spent most of his time preparing his disciples for the inevitable tragedy to come. He was prepared for the excruciating and unbearable pain he'd endure. He was prepared to be whipped and beaten. He knew that he would bleed and cry out for relief. But above all his own demise, he was more concerned for his disciples. He wanted be sure that they were prepared to deal with the agony that would soon rip through their hearts; at the sight of the one they loved and grew to worship being murdered. He wanted to prepare their minds to be wrapped around the idea that the very people he was sent to save, would indeed be the ones to lie, beat him, spit on him, and then crucify him alive.

> He went on, "It is necessary that the Son of Man proceed to an ordeal of suffering, be tried and found guilty by the religious leaders, high priests, and religion scholars, be killed, and on the third day be raised up alive."
>
> **Luke 9:22 The Message Bible**

In the text, the word *"necessary"* implies that Jesus knew there was no other way. As painful, bloody, and frightening as his fate appeared, he stood and accepted His assignment from the Father. Jesus walked and lived a life in tune with the Father. And since the beat of His heart was synchronized to the rhythm of the Father's heart, He knew obedience was his only option.

Jesus was committed unto death to finish the journey that His father had designed for him to complete. Facing abandonment, persecution, being misunderstood, and even a certain agonizing death:

- ❖ He had his *face* set towards Jerusalem.
- ❖ He had his *mind* set on Calvary.
- ❖ He had his *heart* and affections set on "THE CROSS".

Christ took three stands for humanity. He Stood Up! He Stood In! And He stood out!

First, Jesus recognized that he was created for this very purpose: *to stand up*. Jesus did not run from the hellhounds waiting to take away His life. But he stood up and charged right towards the arrows and attacks of the enemy, knowing that he would endure an indescribable pain. It is important to point out here that he was still simply *Jesus*. He was not Jesus "Christ" yet. At this point, in His journey here on Earth, He was not yet clothed in His glory. He was just like you and I. He sweat and bled like us, but he kept going. He cried like us, but he continued loving those who had betrayed him. He became poor like us, but he kept on giving. And as the roman soldiers did their best to beat the life out of him—His body got tired, but he kept standing. In his standing, Jesus stood up for a human race that could not stand up for itself.

Jesus knew that we were a defective and damaged people. Our purity and royalty flawed by sin. But by him offering his sinless life as a living sacrifice, he would indeed stand up for us. He stood on our behalf saying, "I know what they feel, I know their weaknesses, I've experienced their temptations, and it's not easy for them to remain blameless and pure, I understand their pain."

Then he stood out!! Jesus was not the type of guy that would sit back, relax, and enjoy the luxury of being a king. Jesus had 12 disciples whom he could have directed to do whatever he wanted them to do, out of their love for Him, they would have obeyed. He never misused his authority to bring comfort to himself. He always did the opposite of what people expected him to do:

- When everyone was sleeping, he spent late nights and early mornings *praying*.
- When others were hungry, he was *fasting*.
- When people ran from the lepers, he ran *towards* them.
- When the disciples pushed the woman possessed with the demon away, Jesus drew her in, cast the demon out, and set her free.
- When the disciples told the children to step aside, He welcomed them instead.
- When the woman with the issue of blood touched the hem of his garment, he stopped abruptly in a crowd filled with people grabbing for him, and said who touched me??

I am convinced that even the disciples, at times, thought Jesus was strange. But he didn't mind that. Jesus had already accepted that it was his purpose in life to stand out. It was his purpose to be outcast, exiled, and rejected. It was his purpose in life to upset the traditions of humanity. It was his purpose in life to challenge the status quo. It was his purpose to be different.

There were political systems, social classes, and cliques created that too often disqualified Gods' people. They were designed to oppress God's people and discourage them from pursuing their inheritance. They were designed to cause people to feel inferior, invaluable, and ill-equipped.

Many of us make the mistake of thinking that since we have issues, and we all have them... that God cannot use us. We spend too much time counting ourselves out and disqualifying ourselves based on man's measuring stick. Many of us think that our reason for existing is without purpose. But I myself have had to find out the hard way that it is those very issues that God intends to use to create His glory. God will use your mistakes to promote and elevate you.

The bible tells us that, *"without faith it is impossible to please God"* (Heb. 11:6). Most of us cry out, "I want to know my purpose!" Though most of us truly want to please God with our lives, we don't want to go through the pain and the fire to do it. We want to hear the Father say "Well done thy good and faithful servant". But we don't want to feel hurt, abandoned, or rejected. We live in a society where everybody wants to fit in, be accepted, and be a part of something. But when you accept Jesus in your heart and begin to apply God's principles to your everyday life, you will always stand out. When you challenge others to say no to sin, you will stand out. When you do the opposite of what everybody else is doing, you will stand out!!

We as believers are taught that salvation is free. But I must inform you, truthfully, it will cost you *everything*. When you are truly in a loving relationship with the Father you have no choice but to stand up, stand out, and then stand in.

Finally after he stood out for us, *he stood in*. When God created man, He created us to enjoy a perfect and intimate love relationship with Him. Satan had no way of separating us from that love. He had no access to impose on our intimacy and no power over our worship. But, when Adam sinned back in the Garden of Eden, a *gap was created in the gate*. Sin gave Satan the access he needed to come into our lives.

As a result, we became disconnected from our creator. We were no longer one with Him. He was holy and we were sinners—needing the fat of a ram and the blood of a goat to be a remission for our sins. But Jesus said, "No more! I will fill the broken link in the gate so that there can again be a continuous flow of worship between them and the Father".

Jesus stood in the Sanhedrin as the very people he had helped, healed, and loved persecuted him. They lied on, spat on, and beat on Him. But he never said a word—*he just stood in the gap*. Jesus was led up the hill to Calvary, with his flesh beaten and torn, carrying a cross too heavy for one person to carry.

As he walked painfully to his death—*he was standing in the gap*. And after all that, he could have rested for all of eternity in a tomb, wrapped in fine linen. But even then, he got up from his resting place, and kept moving.

After his crucifixion, Jesus, upon arriving at Satan's doorstep, completed the assignment he was created for. He repaired the break in the gate. He became the missing iron link in the gate. *He stood in the Gap!*

See, if Jesus had not made the decision to obey the Father and *stand in* the gap, Satan would still have this entry by which he could continue to wreak havoc in our lives. He would still have power to taint our worship with doubt and disbelief. He would still have the power to cripple our lives with sin. He would still be able to terrorize us with the fear of death.

If Jesus had not stood in the gap, we would continue to be slaves to sin with no way out of our mess. You know the mess like adultery, disease, dysfunction, confusion, jealousy, bitterness, unforgiveness, selfishness, pornography... yeah *all* that mess! But when he stood in the gap and died on the cross, He gave us the authority (and the right) to put our foot on the devil's head, crush it, and then walk away with the victory. Thank you Jesus for standing in the gap!

The Bible tells us that the race is not given to the swift or to the strong, but the reward is given to He that endures 'til the end. (Ecclesiastes 9:11, Matthew 24:13) This means that those that God intends to reward are not those who look at a battle and say, "Oh I got this, I can handle that, look how strong I am! Look how many degrees I have!" or "I've got enough money, I can just buy the battle".

You know some people really think that way. But the reward is not for them. *The reward* is for the subnormal; the average, and the below average; those that feel like they are inadequate. *The reward* is for those that look in the mirror and say "I may not be pretty enough, I may not have enough money, I may not be as strong, I may not quote scripture like the rest of them, but I have a *relationship* with the father and I know He is with me!" *The reward* is for those that can stand and say:

- ❖ "I may not have a car but that's okay, I feel like walking to church."
- ❖ "I may not have fancy suits, but I am going before the King."
- ❖ "I may not have the best of things, but I can offer Him the best of me!!"
- ❖ "I can do all things through Christ who strengthens me."

Are you willing to press forward to obtain your reward? Are you willing to *stand up*, *stand out*, and *stand in* to obtain your reward?

4

Matters of the Heart

Before you begin reading this chapter, I challenge you to do one thing. Sincerely pray and ask God, "Lord show me the current condition of my heart." Things are rapidly changing in our generation. The climate has become has become very hostile. And I am not simply referring to the hurricanes, earthquakes, and tornadoes that have swept across our globe. I am referring to the climate of humanity. Families are drowning in financial hurricanes, businesses have failed due to economic earthquakes and many are caught up in emotional tornadoes—being torn from their foundation in Christ. Things are rapidly changing in the lives of believers. Many key leaders have endured scrutiny by the media. The dynamics of our homes are changing. Our faith in the God and the promises Jesus spoke to us before he was crucified are being challenged on a daily basis.

I can recall a VP I used to work for, I'll just call him Joe here. See even though Joe had emphysema, he refused to quit smoking cigarettes. This man would cough so loud and so hard that you'd believe his heart and lungs were probably lying on the floor back there in his office. One day while I was at work sitting at my desk, Joe walks out of his office and was headed out the building to smoke a cigarette. As he walks past my desk, he sneezes and I say, "Bless you". He sneezes again a second time—I say "Bless you". He sneezes a third time and before I can open my mouth he screams, "I must be allergic to Jesus!!" And everyone in the office is laughing hysterically. But all I can do is shake my head in disbelief.

> "...men's hearts failing them from fear and the expectation of those things that are coming on the earth, for the powers of the heavens will be shaken.
>
> Luke 21:26 NKJV

As funny as that story is, I will never forget the amount of pity I felt for his soul. Imagine that! There are actually people who feel they are *allergic* to Jesus. There are actually people in this generation that fear having a relationship with the Lord may have a negative or adverse reaction on their lives. That is just the world we live in today. There are millions of people who have this twisted idea of salvation. Instead of understanding the positive effect Jesus would have on their lives, they see it as something negative. This is mostly because they are looking at the things they would have to give up, thinking that those things are good for them, like Joes cigarettes. He'd much rather have the cigarettes that are causing cancer and shrinking his infected lungs, than the Saviour that died to set him free from all addictions.

Instead of husbands and wives having meaningful dialogue face to face at the kitchen table or in the bedroom, they engage in important relationship conversation over email, Facebook, and text messages. The success or failures marriages are decided and families are dissolved in the public eye through social media. There was a time when teenage pregnancy was our biggest fear for our children. But that has been replaced by an alarming rate of our children and teens detesting the church, living alternative lifestyles, and committing suicide. Let's look at the prophetic verses below from the book of Hebrews:

> Wherefore (as the Holy Ghost saith, Today if ye will hear his voice, <u>harden not your hearts</u>, as in the rebellion, in the day of temptation in the wilderness: When your fathers tempted me, proved me, and saw my works

forty years. Wherefore I was grieved with that generation, and said, They do always go astray in their heart; and they have not known my ways. So I sware in my wrath, They shall not enter into my rest.) Take heed, brethren, lest there be in any of you an evil heart of unbelief, in departing from the living God. But exhort one another daily, while it is called Today; lest any of you be hardened through the deceitfulness of sin. For we are made partakers of Christ, if we hold the beginning of our confidence steadfast unto the end; While it is said, "Today if ye will hear his voice, <u>harden not your hearts, as in the rebellion."</u>

Hebrews 3:8-13 KJV

As we look at the news and right out of our own front doors, we can clearly see that the times in which we live are filled with sudden tragedy —and for many an uncertain outcome. When our hearts are primed for constant disappointment and trauma, it is very common to find that our hearts have become hardened or calloused. Webster's definition of calloused is: **a:** being hardened and thickened **b:** feeling no emotion. Webster's also lists:

1. a thickening of or a hard thickened area on skin or bark
2. a mass of exudate and connective tissue that forms around a break in a bone and is converted into bone in healing
3. soft tissue that forms over a wounded or cut plant surface

In summary, a callus is an especially toughened area of skin which has become relatively thick and hard in response to *repeated friction, pressure, or other irritation*. Calluses are generally not harmful, but may sometimes lead to other problems, such as skin ulceration or infection.

Are you willing to admit that at some point in your lifetime you have been wounded? Here are some things that can cause repeated friction, pressure and irritation to our hearts:

- Too many failed relationships.
- Repeated rejection by friends and family
- Remaining in toxic or abusive relationships
- Disappointments
- Starting projects but never completing them because of the fear of failure

I would like to elaborate a little further and suggest to you that being calloused is also caused by a constant thirst or desire for something that seems to be unattainable. Like our feet may desire water, moisture, and rest—single people may desire intimate relationship and the comfort of companionship with the opposite sex. Children may desire attention and acceptance from their peers. Men and women both desire praise, recognition, and a sense of achievement. And finally, we all have a thirst and desire to experience an authentic expression of the 4-letter word: LOVE.

In the bible we are warned that our hearts are "deceitful and desperately wicked". (Jer. 17:9). This means that we can be deceived and led down the wrong path when our hearts desire the wrong things. We may feel our motives or intentions are pure, but deep down inside if we did the work we would find out that there was some ulterior self-absorbed motive at work.

For example, you may be offered a great new job, offering double your salary but it would take you away from Sunday worship. The job would require more hours at work and offer less time for studying God's word or family time. Your heart may tell you that it's the right job to take, simply because you are able to provide more for your family. Your heart will even justify it, by reminding you that God requires you to provide and leave an inheritance for your children.

Distracted by the extra money, you make the wrong decision—taking the job and finding out that your spiritual life has become dry and empty. You notice you have become apathetic to worship. You begin to spend Sunday mornings in bed resting instead of running with your family into the church to worship God and give thanks for all His blessings.

No matter how much Satan hates God and his children, no matter how much he frustrates you, Satan cannot destroy you. Satan does not have the power or the authority to create life or take it away. Nor can he stop the work of God in your life. The only power he has is to *distract* and *discourage* you. If you allow him to, his distractions could greatly delay or hinder your journey.

When we constantly strive and push ourselves to obtain the things we desire, it becomes harder to hear the voice of God. We cannot hear God because we are more focused on *that thing* we desire. That's why the scripture says "Today if ye will hear his voice, *harden not your hearts* like they did in the wilderness." (Heb. 3:15)

The Israelites were more focused on the things they felt they deserved and desperately needed so they could not begin to imagine what the Father was doing in their lives. They lost their direction as well as their track of time. So likewise, when it seems as if *that thing* we want is unattainable, when we can't get the things we are thirsty for—we get distracted by the *lack* of it. When we are distracted we have a distorted view of reality. Ultimately, we miss God's plan by making careless mistakes and rushed decisions—then our hearts become hardened and calloused.

I think we can understand now what God meant in the next two scriptures:

"A new heart also will I give you, and a new spirit will I put within you: and I will take away the stony heart out of your flesh, and I will give you an heart of flesh". (Ezekiel 36:26 NKJV)

"For the word of God is quick, and powerful, and sharper than any two-edged sword, piercing even to the dividing asunder of soul and spirit, and of the joints and marrow, and is a discerner of the thoughts and intents of the heart." (Hebrews 4:12 NKJV)

God wants to remove our callused hearts. If our hearts are calloused when the word of God is spoken over our lives, nothing happens. The words are not able to penetrate through the stony exterior wall of our hearts and no change takes place. Unfortunately, we remain unaffected by the voice of God. God wants to replace your hardened heart with a softer heart that can be penetrated by His word.

> Create in me a clean heart, O God; and renew a right spirit within me. "Cast me not away from thy presence; and take not thy holy spirit from me. ¹²Restore unto me the joy of thy salvation; and uphold me with thy free spirit.
>
> Psalm 51:10 KJV

Have you ever taken out a knife and tried to cut a stone? If you've tried, you know that the blade is not going to penetrate that stone no matter how hard you try. God wants to give us a heart that has been softened by His spirit.

When we worship, God is giving us a softer heart; a heart of flesh. He is preparing it to be cut! That's why when we come into the presence of God we must first *worship*. We have to turn our hearts towards Him, and be softened by His love for us—before we deal with the two edged sword. Ask yourself this: Do I want a smooth cut that will heal fast or a jagged cut that will take longer to heal? If He cuts us with His word before we have been prepared, then instead of helping us it would damage us. *Worship is not an option!*

When God searches you, He intends to show you where you really are in your walk with Him. We are like glass to God—He sees it <u>ALL</u>! So be prepared for what you see. It will not be what you expect. It won't be all the great notable victories in your life. No, He is not going to show you the times you fed the hungry, or helped a family member pay a bill. He is not going to show you the time you spent praying or reading your bible. But what He will reveal is where He wants you to grow. He will show you the jealousy in your own heart. He will show you things like greed, jealousy, hidden idolatry, and selfishness. He doesn't present you with a pretty picture. He shows you the ugly truth as He sees it.

But the blessing comes by knowing that the same God who created you and started a great assignment through your life, will keep on working at any cost to complete it! (Phil 1:6) He won't leave us that way. He will keep molding you as long as you live...until He can see an image of Himself *in you*!

Who is *Lord* at the center of your heart? Who governs your decisions? When you ask God to search your heart, and purge it, you must be prepared. God will show you who you have truly made Lord in your life. Is it food, your spouse, or recognition? Is it fine clothing? Is it that pipe or the bottle? Is it marijuana? Is it money? Is it sex? The very thing that creates conflict between you and God causes you to lose interest in God and wants to be Lord. Who is really Lord?

Some of you may be asking, "What about the mind? What do I do when my heart wants to do the wrong thing and the mind is telling me to do what's right?" That is a classic question! Even the Apostle Paul encountered this dilemma.

But even more so, you may be asking, "What are some practical things we can do to synchronize our heart with what our mind says is the "right thing" to do?

First, the most important thing and the hardest thing we can ever learn to do is *confess*! Now I know this is not a tasty word to chew on, but I've tasted it and I've survived many confessions. You can too! Confess that sin that you know you are repeatedly faced with. You know *the one!* In order for change to occur we must confront the issue. The longer you retreat and attempt to hide from the truth, the harder your heart becomes.

The next thing I can suggest is for you to figure out how to *wait*. Patience, endurance, and self-control are all fruits of walking in the spirit and must be practiced while waiting.

Whatever it is you are waiting for, *how* you wait will reveal the condition of your heart. You have not mastered waiting, if you are waiting and complaining, waiting and anxious, or waiting and afraid. I realized I needed to grow in the area of waiting when I found myself trying to be the god of my own life. Like many others, I would get involved and try to help God move things along. I was trying to help God *be God*. God doesn't need my help!

I know what it's like for God to tell me to wait for something, but instead turn to other vices to remove the sting of waiting. I had not conquered my anxieties and my fears so I turned to sex, alcohol, drugs, and shopping. But I heard God calling out to me, "I want your heart!! I want your heart!!" What I have learned is that when you master waiting on the Father to move, then you will no longer focus on *the thing* and Satan cannot distract you with your anxieties for having it.

Since we are created in the image of God, it is imperative that we work to reflect the exact same image of His heart. As we make our home in Him, we find the courage to withstand our greatest trials. As we make our home in Him, our affections and desires become parrallel to His. As we make our home in Him, His love flows freely to heal every pain and calm every fear. If His heart has this effect in us, then shouldn't our hearts have this same effect on others?

5

Prevail and Excel

Not enough times in our lives do we hear the encouraging words needed to motivate us to keep pushing forward. So in this book, my goal is to encourage you to rise above whatever you think is your darkest moment. You have done so much of the *work of faith* that at this point in your life you have become a fortress of faith for others. The very reason this book is written is to tell you this: God is well pleased with you. He is well pleased with how you stood in the midst of your storms. You have not lost hope in His promises. You have actually grown and matured in your ability to look beyond the darkness. The storms you have managed to survive this far, were not easy victories. It has taken *everything* in you to run this race. It took endurance for you to not lose your mind. You have had to press beyond your fears and doubts. At times you felt like giving up and quitting. As a matter of fact many of you have even said, "I quit!" But His *grace* has kept you. After all you have been through, even after you gave up and threw in the towel, His grace has kept you! And here you are: Still standing!! So don't let anyone belittle your testimony. Don't let anyone devalue your victory! God wants you to know, your ability to have survived that storm, makes you a champion. You *are* a champion!! Repeat after me: I *am* a champion!!

I am confident in saying that in spite of everything the enemy does to try and destroy you, in the end you will prevail. In spite of the mistakes you have made—you are still valuable! In spite of the failed attempts you are still qualified for greatness!

God promises that in this next chapter of your life:

- You will *<u>triumph</u>* –which is the joy or exultation of victory or success. Get your praise dance ready! God is restoring your joy.

- You will *<u>succeed</u>* –which means things are designed to turn out well for you.

- You will *<u>overcome</u>* –which means you will gain superiority. You will rise above your inadequacies. You will rise above your enemy's attacks.

- You will *<u>reign</u>* –which means you will walk in royal authority: You will take authority over the things, the people, and the systems which once controlled you.

- You will *<u>abound</u>* – which means you will no longer be outnumbered by the people or things that have been working against you.

- You will *<u>rule</u>* –which means you will control, govern, and be in power—over the issues that have hindered your growth (gambling, drugs, alcohol, sex, debt, etc.)

Declare this aloud: I will triumph! I will succeed! I will overcome! I will reign! I will abound! I will RULE!!!

In addition to prevailing, you will also excel. When I use the word excel here I am saying that:

- You will <u>perform extremely well</u>
- You will <u>shine</u> in the midst of darkness
- You will <u>stand out</u> from those who have made you common
- You will <u>surpass</u> those who have not endured the testing

- ❖ You will <u>outclass</u> those who rely on material things to define them
- ❖ You will <u>outrival</u> those who said you wouldn't make it.

> *For when God made a promise to Abraham, because He could swear by no one greater, He swore by Himself, saying "Surely blessing I will bless you, and multiplying I will multiply you. And so after he had patiently endured, he obtained the promise!"*
>
> **Hebrews 6:11-13 NKJV**

How did Abraham endure? He endured patiently! What happened next? He obtained the promise! To summarize Abraham's experience, I feel safe concluding that "patience gets the promise!

Many of us here in the western hemisphere expect to experience no more than the natural progression of life: school, college, marriage, jobs, raise the kids, and now sadly increasing in our generation: divorce. Many people have been accustomed (and satisfied) with that. But then there are a few of us who wake up each morning, or come home after a long day's work, and as our heads fall in our hands we hear that voice, within us crying out, "There has got to be more to my existence than this!!"

Nobody wants to endure the painful process of pruning that God requires of us. I don't know about you, but I have experienced the panful effects of losing a wrestling match with God. While pursuing my own ambitions, I started out with the best intentions and I created my strategic plans for success. But somewhere along the way God stepped into my plans and showed me His plan—and then I wrestled with His plan! See when I created my plan, I had no idea that there was so much more that God wanted to perfect in my life.

In the year 2011, I went through the most excruciating wrestling match with God. I am sure you already you know who won that match. I experienced so much warfare, transition, and disappointment that I asked God, "What is 2011 all about???" So He led me to do a little research.

- ❖ The number 11 is a prime number.
- ❖ It can only be divided by one and itself.

- There are no other relevant factors.
- The number 11 is read the same backwards and forwards.
- If you turn an 11 sideways it turns into an "equal to sign" (=) and the characters on each side of the "equal to" sign must be the same.
- Therefore, the number 11 represents a *mirror* in the spirit.

The year 2011 was the year of my mirror. When you look in a mirror it will always give you an authentic reflection. The mirror may be clean or dirty, but the reflection is the same. What you see is what you get!!

That year, I truly learned that this life we live is not about getting "stuff". See many of us have been wrestling with God over material things. But in retrospect, He has been wrestling with us over *His* will. All along, the war has been about getting us to delight in *His will* for our lives.

Most times, unless He shows us a new house, a new car, or a new job—we don't delight in the things God has in store for us. The reason we don't instantly delight in His will over our own, is because it is always preceded by a sacrifice. Yes, God wants us to release something! It might be a car, it might be a plan, and it might be regret or forgiving someone who has hurt us. But God wants us to delight in doing His will—even if that means releasing the very thing that we don't want to release.

> Death and Life are in the power of the tongue: and they that love it shall eat its fruit.
>
> **Proverbs 18:21 NKJV**

But if you will allow Him, God will mature your faith and bring you to a place where you will delight in whatever He calls you to do!! After surviving the battles in our relationships, our finances, and in our homes…God is calling us to open our hands, finger by finger, and let go!

I am convinced that God wants to develop such obedience in us that we easily release anything that does not line up with where He is taking us. So the things and people you think you lost—don't look back at that. Look forward.

Look towards the direction God is taking you. That is the only way you will walk in your purpose. Paul Said, "For the sufferings of the current age, are not worthy to be compared to the glory which is to come." (Rom 8:18) If you have found yourself growing and getting good at releasing these things that keep you out of God's divine purpose, watch out! *Glory is coming!!*

The first and most important (yet practical) thing we must learn to do is to align *our words* with *His words*. The book of Proverbs tells us that *what* we speak has the power of producing life or death.

You used to disqualify yourself by speaking words of doubt. You used to kill your ability to be fruitful by repeating all the negative words that have been spoken over your life. But by now, God expects us to start repeating back to Him what He has already spoken. When God speaks a word of life over us, He is planting a seed. He then expects you to water that seed. When you repeat His words back to Him you are watering the seeds God has planted in you. A seed cannot grow without water. And if you are not repeating back to Him what was spoken, you are blocking your own growth.

The next practical thing we must learn to do is discipline our thoughts to line up with His thoughts. In order to do this we must endure the stripping away of old ideas, old insecurities, and old regrets. So this way when we think, we are of the same mind with Him. If God has forgotten your mistakes, then you must forget them as well. Take note of the scriptures below:

- ❖ The apostle Paul says, "Let this mind be in you, which was also in Christ Jesus." (Phil. 2:5)

- ❖ God tells us that, "For my thoughts are not your thoughts, neither are your ways my ways, saith the LORD."(Isaiah 55:8)

- ❖ Solomon instructs us, "Commit thy works unto the LORD, and thy thoughts shall be established." (Prov 16:3)

- ❖ David says, "How precious also are thy thoughts unto me, O God! How great is the sum of them."(Psalm 139:17)

- ❖ David says, "LORD, how great are thy works! And thy thoughts are very deep." (Psalm 92:5)

❖ God tells Jeremiah, "For I know the thoughts that I think toward you, saith the LORD, thoughts of peace, and not of evil, to give you an expected end." (Jer.29:11)

So ask yourself this, "What am I thinking??" In the story of the prodigal son, once the son got so far away from everything He knew to be right he found himself having dinner with pigs. And then, he had a moment when he came to himself. He said at that moment, "I will arise and go to my father." (Lk.15:11-32) Won't you join in with me in this declaration?

"We declare before you today God, We have come to ourselves!! We will arise and come to you!!!"

That same year, the most valuable lesson I learned was that in order to discover God's purpose for my life, I must line up with His ways. Many people ask the question, "What is my purpose?" A simple answer is this: Our lives are created to give God glory. That's it! So in all of the trials we face, God's goal is to mold us, shape us, and reform us to look like Him. God resurrects our dreams and the things He has created us to accomplish. Once we accept that it is *HIS* purpose (and not our own) to fulfill, then we are going somewhere! But first, He has to clean us up.

And to start things off, He will initiate the cleaning process by increasing our appetite for worship. In a dry and weary land—during the recession, after the rejection, after the divorce—He will increase our thirst for Him. There, we discover that it makes no sense to try and impress folk (who don't really like us anyway), or try to create this flawless and superficial image. Everybody goes through or is going through something—that is just the truth! When He increases our appetite for Him, and we begin to go after a closer relationship with Him, then we will become a threat to the enemy. That is when we really experience hardship. And it is during hardship, that God works to mold us into His image.

People are going to talk about you if you are doing well—they are going to talk when you struggle. So it just makes sense to just stay in His grace, stay in His will, and walk according to His ways. It just makes more sense to "delight" in His will. Our response to God's command should be, "*Yes Father I'd be delighted to.*" David says:

- ❖ I delight to do thy will, O my God: yea, Thy law is within my heart. (Psalm 40:8 kjv)

- ❖ The steps of a good man are ordered by the LORD: and he delights in his way. (Psalm 37:23 kjv)

When Jesus was preparing go to the cross, he spent a little time in the garden. In his humanism, Jesus begged the Father to "Please *take this cup from me*". After several hours of praying, crying, and sweating blood, he gets to the place where he declares to God, "*Nevertheless* not my will. But Thy will be done!"

It is important to note that for quite some time you have been in the garden. God Has been wrecking all the methods you have been accustomed to getting things done. He has been painfully prying people, ideas, and things away from us. He has allowed us to fall and get back up again repeatedly. He has been destroying *your* carefully crafted blueprint for life. He has been destroying your comfort zone.

And now, after all *your* attempts to do things *your* way, like me you have said, "Okay God, It is what it is!" Since you've finally accepted the call of God on your life (for real), you've noticed that you are no longer easily accepted by the people you used to call friends. Your phone has stopped ringing as much and you don't get invitations to hang out with the old crew anymore. You've begun to realize you must hold yourself to a much higher standard of living. And that causes everything in your life to begin shifting into alignment with that call.

During a very dark season in my life, I experienced this type of isolation. I heard the spirit of God say, "*Kimberly, but if you delight yourself to do My will, I will give you the desires of your heart.*" This meant I had to lay down my own will, agendas, timelines, and methods and truly *seek* His will. This meant that the answers and the relationships I sought after may not come in my time.

This meant I could not create my own plans and deadlines for turning things around. But I had to wait on Him! I had to surrender my heart, my fears, and my doubts to *His will* and *His timing*. In doing so, I found myself enjoying the quiet, quality time alone with the Lord—learning to totally trust, lean, and depend on Him. When you delight yourself in His will for your life, you will begin to see God's hand moving, and your prayers being answered.

Many of you understand that the number 12 represents *foundation* and *government*. As you work to enter the next phase of your life, it is very important that you have allowed God to lay a firm foundation for His purposes to be fulfilled. It is best described by comparing fulfilling your life's purpose to building a great mansion. When I think of myself and all that God has created me to fulfill in this life, I envision a huge mansion.

How do you see yourself? Do you see a small shabby home with only one door? Or do you envision the greatness God has designed for you? Let me just say this, if you are like me and you are dreaming of mansions and estates, your life's work will require a strong foundation. What good is a beautiful home built without columns or beams and standing on sand? What good is your life's work, if on the inside you are empty, broken, and depressed? If a stronger and much more durable foundation is not built, when the next wave of storms arise your life you will be left in ruins—waiting to be rebuilt again. And who really wants to repeat this process?

Before you begin the building phase, here are some key points about your house that you will need to remember:

- ❖ Paul says, "Your body is the temple of the Holy Ghost which is in you, which you have of God, and you are not your own."(*1 Cor. 6:19*)
- ❖ Jesus tells us that, "A house divided against itself cannot stand." (*Mark 3:25*)
- ❖ James tells us that, "a double minded man is unstable in all his ways."(*James 1:8*)
- ❖ King Solomon tells us, "Unless God builds the house they labor in vain that Build it." (*Psalm 127:1*)
- ❖ And Joshua declared, "As for me and my house, we will serve the Lord!"(*Joshua 24:15*)

> *Delight yourself in the Lord, and He will give you the desires of your heart.*
> **Psalm 37:4 ESV**

By the time you begin walking in all that God has called you to, you should be able to see what He sees when you look in the mirror. You should be saying what He says. You should be thinking what He thinks.

Each and every day you should be getting up and looking in the mirror and declaring that, "I am fearfully and wonderfully made! I am a mighty man of valor! I am a phenomenal woman! I am clothed in righteousness and honor! I am a champion! There is a great plan for my life and God has already completed it!"

I am convinced that there are future business leaders, and future community leaders reading this book right now. So I challenge you today, don't miss the boat and get left behind. Get ready and get delighted! You are about to walk out the plans God has already drawn for you to live your life to the fullest! Your labor during the storm has not been in vain. It was only because of His blood and His grace that you have come this far. His grace has been made sufficient in your weakness!! Jesus and Jesus alone still and always will be the reason you are still standing. God has built a mansion for you! There is now a strong foundation of faith in you. And you will be able to stand the test of time. You are ready to run! Nothing and nobody can hinder you now. You are fully capable of pursuing and recovering all that God has in store for you. Don't look back! And don't try to skip today. But each day you wake up, spring forth and declare to the world, "*I will PREVAIL and I will EXCEL!!!*"

6

Jesus Saved Us All...

Not too frequently, do we get excited about dark gray skies and cloudy days. It is our nature to prefer to feel the heat of the sun and stare into "daydream worthy" blue skies filled with clouds like pillows. We look forward to cool spring breezes and the crisp air of fall. But when the daydream ends and we find ourselves back in reality, we are forced to accept that many of our days are filled with thunderstorms and heavy floods of rain. The Bible describes two different rains the former rain and the latter rain (aka the *last* rain and the *next* rain).

And the latter rain shall be greater than the former rain. Would you just stop for a minute and just say this out loud? "My best days are yet to come!" No matter what you think you have accomplished or what tragedy you just barely escaped in your past—God has something even greater up ahead in store for your life.

There is a reason He allowed you to survive. There is a reason the police didn't catch you. There is a reason that your body has not given in to the attack of AIDS and cancer. There is a reason the divorce didn't kill you.

God still intends to bless you. There is work for you to do that will have an impact on somebody else's life. You have not lived your best days yet.

But beware, between the rains—*between the former and the latter*, there is a desert. After the former rain and before the next heavy rain of blessings, the writer does not think it is important to mention that there is a period of no rain. The period of no rain, the desert, is a place of sacrifice. This is the place where your faith will be tested. This is the period of your life where you think people have forgotten who you are.

During this time of no rain—you will even begin to question what was it all for? Why did God bring me out here to this place so far from everything I was accustomed to—*for me to die?*

> Therefore be patient, brethren, until the coming of the Lord. See how the farmer waits for the precious fruit of the earth, waiting patiently for it until it receives the early and the latter rain.
>
> **James 5:7 NKJV**

If you can recall, Jesus was baptized by John and all who were around witnessed the heavens opening as he was declared the beloved Son of God. And soon after, Jesus performed all of his glorious miracles, becoming famous as people near and far heard of his parables, his wisdom and the healing power in his hands.

He became a highly sought after celebrity among mankind as people heard how he walked on top of the sea and how he could speak to the winds for them to obey his commands. But after his baptism and before his rise to fame, he entered the wilderness for 40 days. He entered his desert—a place of no rain.

While Jesus was in the desert, he was in the company of wild beasts. In the desert there are hungry and thirsty wild coyotes lurking to and fro looking for flesh to devour. If you can recall, before *Job entered His* desert, Satan told God He was *"roaming 'to and fro' looking for a soul to devour." (Job 1:7)*

It is very important to note that when you are in a spiritual desert there are coyotes lurking; watching and waiting for you to throw in the towel. They are waiting for you to fall out in exasperation. They patiently wait until you give in to exhaustion. Spiritual coyotes wait for you to exhaust all of your ideas, and you no longer have the energy to fight off an attack. They cleverly disguise themselves as harmless. You never recognize their existence until you have given in. As soon as you do they will come and easily claim their prey. But during the course of his stay in the wilderness, Jesus was ministered to by the angels. Though he was tempted and taunted by Satan, God sent His angels to comfort Him *even in the desert*. Jesus is our human example of what it is like to actually go through a dry season and actually come out of it with more power than when he went in.

Some people view Jesus as a magician—performing miracles that would never be done again. But Jesus was not a magician. He simply *was not*. He did not walk the earth in his spiritual form. Jesus was a human man born in flesh, like you and I. What made him different was the fact that He *understood*, He *accepted*, and He *believed* who God said He was! And that belief gave him POWER!!

After Jesus overcame his desert experience, he began to produce rivers of living water. When will you start believing what God spoke about you? When you start believing what God says about you, a shift begins to take place. And that shift will begin to take place in your mind as you start to thinking about victory. Instead of focusing on the storm, all you can begin to see is yourself on the other side.

> Rivers of living water shall flow from within the hearts of them that believe.
>
> John 7:38 NIV

Then a shift takes place in your heart. Instead of feeling the pain of despair, faith arises and comes alive inside of you. Every beat that your heart takes beats to the rhythm of faith in knowing you are loved. With all this faith, hope, and love growing inside, you find yourself walking 10 feet taller. And with your head held high—your entire walk changes! You begin to walk with confidence, as if you have already seen the manifestation!

A shift takes place in your attitude. Now don't let this catch you off guard, but people will think you are crazy. Some will be convinced that you have gone bananas! But it won't matter to you because, you will have begun to understand and believe what it truly means to have the favor of God on your life. And when you believe, you begin to operate in the *law of attraction.*

The law of attraction states (in summary) that you can only attract what is on the inside of you. That means: *When you believe, you begin to attract what you believe on the inside.* When you believe what God has spoken to you about yourself—*nobody* can tell you anything that contradicts what God has spoken.

Mass media outlets have created the perception that a smaller sized woman is more beautiful that a woman that would be classified as obese.
By no means am I glorifying obesity. I firmly believe that God calls all of us to honor Him in the way we manage our bodies. But I know several overweight men and women who have heard a voice from God that says, "I love you and you are beautiful or handsome in my sight!" And do you know that since they caught wind of God saying they are beautiful and actually *believed* it—nobody can tell them anything different?

I have witnessed it—in fact, there are many people who are extremely overweight who have much higher self-esteem than some smaller individuals. *Why*? Because in order to gain self-confidence, they stopped making it about what *the world* says is beautiful or handsome, and they began to believe what *God* said about them! This is why you see couples and people will question, "How did <u>she</u> get that handsome guy?" or "How did <u>he</u> get such a beautiful woman?" The person whom society had classified as unattractive had an unwavering belief on the inside that, "I am beautiful, I am gorgeous, I am handsome!" And because of the law of attraction – that's exactly what they attracted!

Many times God gives us a revelation about ourselves, and before we can get up out of bed to start the day, we have begun rationalizing what God said. We either begin to talk ourselves out of what God has spoken, or we begin to discredit what was spoken! If we can't make logical sense of it then we write it off. We allow the media and naysayers around us to talk us back out of what God spoke about us.

But you need to begin to expect the abundance of rain. God says for you to *expect* an overflow of favor!! Get past the desert and *believe* that God has a plan for your life. During the desert experience, we are tested of our faith and our ability to endure pain.

Jesus endured this desert place in his life *before* the season of performing great miracles. Jesus wept. But he could endure the pain of being rejected by the community. He could endure the pain of rejection—because He had already conquered being alone...*in the desert*!!

> So if anyone who cleanses himself of what is unfit, he will be a vessel for honor: sanctified, useful to the Master and prepared for every good work.
>
> 2 Timothy 2:21 BIB

When Jesus offered living water to the Samaritan woman at the well, He never promised that she wouldn't face hard times again. But he assured her that if she drank from his well of living water, she would not thirst again, *not even in a desert*. Many don't want to go thru the desert. Most of us would do anything to avoid the dry season of rejection, lack, abandonment, and being misunderstood by everyone we know. For this very cause, most of us *despise* the desert. For this cause, many take their own lives physically and/or spiritually and simply don't survive the desert.

Nobody wants to be rejected, cast out, talked about, and left alone. But for those that do survive it, they recognize that the desert experience is a vital part of their spiritual development. The desert experience is a pre-requisite for being fit for the Master's use.

Every time Satan lied and tried to attack Jesus' belief, Jesus was tested. The word in him was tested. His relationship with the Father was tested! Each time he declared, "It is written" in essence He was saying to the devil, "I know what I'm doing and why I'm doing it, and you can't talk me out of it!"

Jesus was not only tested with hunger and fame. In the desert Jesus was tested of his emotional intelligence.

*[1]Emotional intelligence is the capacity of individuals to recognize their own, and other people's emotions, to discriminate between different feelings and label them appropriately, and to use emotional information to guide thinking and behavior.

If we don't go through the testing in the desert, then we won't have the spiritual maturity and emotional intelligence to make it through to the next phase of our spiritual journey. If Jesus had not gone through the emotional test in the desert, he would not have conquered the cross with such grace and humility.

After going through the desert and claiming the victory there, there is nothing that the enemy could throw at Jesus that he would not be able to face. Many of you right now are going through a desert experience. It seems as if all your wells have dried up. But if you are reading this book, I am announcing to you today that it's time to overcome the desert. It's time for the *latter* rain.

After his desert experience, Jesus began to walk in his latter rain. So let's see—who did Jesus save on his way to the cross?

1. Jesus overcame the death of Lazarus. Even when others thought he had arrived too late to save him, he only spoke and Lazarus came walking out of his tomb.

2. Peter and the other professional fishermen sat in a boat all night long and caught no fish. But Jesus gets on the boat with his solid belief system and the fisherman begin to catch so much fish that the nets began to break!

3. The woman with the issue of blood had been ill for 12 long years, but that was no match for Jesus. She only touched him—and by her faith he made her whole.

Because Jesus simply believed what God said about him, he was a walking reservoir of God's blessings! No matter what people were experiencing before Jesus showed up, after being in his presence, many times only for a short moment, they realized, *It is well!* On his way to be crucified on the cross Jesus told His mother, "*It is well*". The night before his capture, He told the disciples, "*It is well.*" And likewise for you—*It is well*!!

Even as Jesus traveled to the cross he was able to say in essence, "This is the day that the Lord has made; I will rejoice and be glad in it." If he had not endured and come through the desert he would not have made it through the pain at the cross. If he had not gone through the dry season he would have exhausted on the way. He would not have survived the journey there.

His arms stretched wide and horizontal on the cross represents our need for one another. God never intended for us to be alone. Some of you feel like, you are out in the desert alone. But God says, "You are not alone, I have sent my people to love you." Stay connected to other believers. Those who are truly successful have come through their deserts with a divine connectivity to others.

His body hanging vertically on the cross was a symbol of the gift of relationship God has given us. God says, "No matter what you go through, don't ever leave me." Don't ever leave God. He will never leave you. When it feels as though the world has turned its back on you in the desert, He is right there. Jesus said, "I am the vine and you are the branches, apart from me you can do nothing." *(John 15:5)*

I don't care what you feel oppressed by—*nothing* shall become a wall between you and God's love. You've always got that! And because you've got His love, you are strong. You can dream again. You can live! You can thrive!

The Lord is your Shepherd. It is not possible for you have a want that the Shepherd cannot fulfil. You shall want for nothing! So move forward from this desert and enjoy the latter rain. Move on to greater days! Let go of yesterday, your mistakes, and the hurt. It's a new day! Enjoy the *latter rain*!!

7

Confidence to Press Forward

As the Angel led Lot and his family out of Sodom and Gomorrah, right before GOD destroyed it, He told them not to take one look back. His wife disobeyed and was killed instantly. He told them not to look back because there are just some *former things* God wants us to forget. But as He is leading the Israelites out of Egypt the Lord tells them to look back once more. What's different here? Take a look at the passages below:

❖ Here, God says, "Don't look back."

Lot was dragging his feet. The men grabbed Lot's arm, and the arms of his wife and daughters—God was so merciful to them!—and dragged them to safety outside the city. When they had them outside, Lot was told, <u>"Now run for your life! Don't look back!</u> Don't stop anywhere on the plain—run for the hills or you'll be swept away." (Genesis 19:16-17 The MSG Bible)

❖ But here, God says, "Take one last look back."

Moses spoke to the people: "Don't be afraid. Stand firm and watch God do His work of salvation for you today. <u>Take a good look back</u> at the Egyptians today for you're never going to see them again. (Exodus 14:13 The MSG Bible)

In both cases, God wants Lot's family and the Israelites to remember where He has delivered them from. Too many times we look back and get captivated and caught up in our past. We look back and get entangled in old relationships and old habits. We start feeling those old emotions again. When we look back our senses get involved and we remember the taste, the smell, the sound, the visual and the feelings of our past. Looking back makes it harder for us to *change*. Reliving the good feelings and moments make it difficult for us to let go of yesterday. God is saying here that, "Sometimes it is dangerous, even *fatal* for you to look back".

> 44 And so God gave Israel the entire land that he had solemnly vowed to give to their ancestors. They took possession of it and made themselves at home in it. And God gave them rest on all sides, as he had also solemnly vowed to their ancestors. Not a single one of their enemies was able to stand up to them—God handed over all their enemies to them.
>
> **Joshua 21:44 The Message Bible**

But this time when you look back, it's different. This time when you look back you are to recognize this: the weapons that were formed against you, <u>*they did not prosper!*</u> The *divorce*, it didn't prosper, the *debt*—it didn't prosper, the *rape*—it didn't prosper, the *AIDS*—it didn't prosper, the *jail time*—it didn't prosper!!

God wants you to look back at all of the things He brought you out of and have a WOW moment! When I look back over my life, I recognize that there are things that I never could have imagined I would experience. And when I had the experience, I never thought I would survive. Many times I thought, "Kimberly, just give up, this is where the road ends for you". And in fact, I truly wanted to *give up*.

I entertained suicidal thoughts like, "Well would they miss you if you weren't here anymore? Could the kids survive this world without you?" Tired of the disappointments, lies, and attack—I sat on the side of my bed many nights and considered just packing my bags and running away. But the "weapons of mass destruction" in my life—*they did not prosper!!* My spiritual mother, Mrs. Kathy, looked me in my face and said "Kimberly, there are many more adventures for you. God will give you many more stories to tell." At that very moment something leaped in me. Something moved. *Something changed!!*

God has shown us time after time in the bible, that we should not fear our enemies—for they are powerless against us. Therefore we can simply "love them and leave them to the Lord". Some people just say "love them and leave them". But I must point out that it is important to not just *leave them*, but *leave them to the Lord.* Give them totally over to God in prayer. Many people have no-one praying for them- which is why they have been led down a path filled with so much hurt, anger, and abuse.

Believe it or not, the hurt and abuse does not begin with them abusing you. It begins on the inside—as they abuse themselves out of low self-esteem. As a result, what happens on the inside of them happens on the outside. As they abuse themselves, they abuse others—because this has become their norm. But if *you* leave them to the Lord in prayer, then He can begin to do His work in their lives. There are some people who have come through your life, whom you may safely leave the Lord. They are now a part of your past, and God has so many more adventures for you.

There are people who have persecuted you, lied on you, abandoned you, abused and betrayed you—and left you for dead!! But God has delivered you out of the hands of them all. Because of His protection, they are no longer able to stand up against you. Those that fought you with all their strength, fighting to see you fall—they are no longer able to stand up to you. When you begin to walk in the anointing, the power, and the love God placed in you, your *enemies* will recognize it as well.

Do you know that along with prayer, *love* is the most powerful weapon God gave you? God put you through all of that turmoil to break you—so that once you were broken He could pour His love *in you*. Hurt and offense is a vicious cycle, because hurting people continue to hurt other innocent people. Once someone has been emotionally hurt, it is important for them to forgive and release the offense as quickly as possible. If they never receive the healing power of God in their hearts and let the offense go, the heart becomes hardened.

With a hardened heart, they lose that natural ability to genuinely love and be loved. They are now cold-hearted and empty—a perfect host for the enemy. Walking in unforgiveness gives the enemy power over your life. See the enemy can't enter into a heart that is full of God's love; there is no room for him. But when you are waking up each day forgiving, showing mercy, and having joy because you are full of God's love, the enemy knows that the spirit of offense is no longer in you. Therefore, he can no longer take up residence in you. He can no longer use you to hurt others.

After spending countless years living a broken life because of the abuse that I have experienced, I have found that love is the key to being truly free. LOVE = FREE. The enemy would have you to think that showing love to people who have hurt you makes you look weak or like a doormat.

But I am here to tell you, when you are walking in love you are actually demonstrating strength. It takes a strong person to love those who have abused them. It takes strength and courage to forgive those who have hurt you even if they have not recognized what they did was wrong. This has proven to be my hardest life lesson to learn. Many of the people who have hurt me, abused me, or abandoned me don't think they did anything wrong. But one by one God helped me to release the hurt and pain. God allowed me to see them as He sees them. He still loves them and so should I. And as a result of loving the unlovable, I discovered the peace that comes as a reward of letting people go.

I can actually look myself in the mirror each morning and with *boldness* say "If God would be for you, then who would dare be against you?!" David declared, "The Lord is my light and my salvation, of whom shall I fear?? The Lord is the strength of my life, of whom shall I be afraid?" So to you my dear readers, it's our time to rise in the love and strength of the Lord. It's time for you to "*be strong in the Lord and in the power of His might*". It's time for you to lift up your heads and shout, "*I made it!*" "*I survived the storm!*" "*I am still here!*"

> I press toward the mark for the prize of the high calling of God in Christ Jesus.
>
> **Philippians 3:14 NKJV**

Paul was speaking of a prize that he had never seen with his natural eye. Yet though he had not seen it, he went after it with everything he had—even until death. Paul had an assurance on the inside of him that there was a prize to be obtained. He had an assurance that there was something of greater value than all the drama and distress he had seen and been through. Something made the journey worth traveling.

I love the way that same scripture is written in the message bible:

> 12-14 I'm not saying that I have this all together, that I have it made. But I am well on my way, reaching out for Christ, who has so wondrously reached out for me. Friends, don't get me wrong: By no means do I count myself an expert in all of this, but I've got my eye on the goal, where God is beckoning us onward–to Jesus. I'm off and running, and I'm not turning back.
> (Philippians 3:12-14 The MSG Bible)

Hebrews 11:6 tells us that "those that come to the Father must believe that He exists and that He is a rewarder of them that earnestly and diligently seek Him." Note that it *did not* say, "He will reward those that diligently seek things." It did not say "He will reward those who seek the job, the car, the house, the friendships, the husband or the wife". We must be seeking *HIM*. And to seek Him means to put every other thing and agenda aside and going in the direction that leads to Him. That means saying no to the things that don't please Him. That means forsaking all others for HIM—which simply put means to put God first. That means getting down on your face day after day—night after night and crying out to God—telling Him, "Have your way God! Do what you want to do! Change what you want to change—take away whatever you want to take away! I've done doing things my way, I've done things despite your directions and made a mess of things. Now God have your way—wash me, cleanse me, purify my heart, make me new!"

Matthew 6:33 says, "Seek ye first the Kingdom of God and all His righteousness and all these things shall be added unto you." If the Kingdom of God is in us, then His righteousness is in us. Therefore, He must mean for us to seek His righteousness –which is *in us*. Isn't it interesting that God would have us to seek after something that we already have on the inside of us? What's even more interesting to me is that people seek all their lives and never find the thing that was with them all along. See, the enemy would condemn you, if you even dared to think there is something *good* in you. He would have you to think you are worthless rags. But that's a lie!

Yes we were all born into sin. Sin is missing the mark. But if the mark of the high calling is *in* you, then *sin* is going after anything which is not already *in* you! Every time you hope for, pursue, or try to become something that you are not you are in *sin*.

The good news is that the moment you made the decision to come into a relationship with Christ and accept Him as Lord over your life, you changed the course of the wind. That very moment you evicted the power of sin and in return you invited the Holy Spirit and "God's righteousness" to move in and have His way in you. Paul said in Corinthians, "Do you not know that that your body is the temple of the Holy Ghost which is in you, which ye have of God, and ye are not your own?" So, no, you might not have it all together. Yes you have flaws, but there *is* something good in you. And when you go after that good thing that is in you, then you will enter the abundant life Jesus came for you to live! When you go after what He put in you, your soul begins to prosper. 3 James 1:2 says, *"Beloved I wish that you would prosper, and be in good health, even as your soul prospers!!"*

> So do not throw away your confidence. It will be richly rewarded.
>
> **Hebrews 10:35 NIV**

What is confidence? *₂Webster's states that, confidence is,
a. a feeling or consciousness of one's powers, and
b. the quality or state of being certain.

The first definition does not merely refer to one's own power absent of God. But it does refer to the power which was invested in us by the Holy Spirit. That power is a gift. The second definition merely states that *confidence* is an assurance.

How many of you have the assurance that God will never leave you nor forsake you? When you are confident and assured that you are not alone, you can rest. With that assurance you don't have to try to work things out by your own strength or might. But you are able to rest assured in the safety of His spirit! When you are resting *assured*, you don't have to walk the floor at night worrying.

Let's take a look at what God says about the living promise:

> *We received the same promises as those people in the wilderness, but the promises didn't do them a bit of good because they didn't receive the promises with faith. If we believe, though, we'll experience that state of resting. But not if we don't have faith, remember that God said,*
> *"Exasperated, I vowed,"They'll never get where they're going, never be able to sit down and rest." So this promise has not yet been fulfilled. Those earlier ones never did get to the place of rest because they were disobedient. God keeps renewing the promise and setting the date as today...*
> *(Hebrews 4:1-3, 4-6 MSG Bible)*

And so this is still a living promise. It wasn't canceled at the time of Joshua; otherwise, God wouldn't keep renewing the appointment for "today." The promise of "arrival" and "rest" is still there for God's people. God Himself is at rest. And at the end of the journey we'll surely rest with God. But even when we are living our lives obedient to God's word, we can rest. When you discipline your life to do what is right, you don't have to look over your shoulder and worry about your enemies coming after you. God promises that if we forgive and freely cancel the debts of others, He will do the same for us.

God is proud of you, no matter how you finished the race. God is proud of you because you continued to run. The devil wanted you to quit. He did everything he could to discourage you. But God put you on a course perfectly carved out for you to win. And He put His Spirit in you to push you to the finish line, even after you threw in the towel! If you are like me, I have given up the race many times on this journey, but that only pushed me along further. It pushed me further because each time *I quit* and refused to run, His spirit took over, and carried me much further than I could have gone on my own. God's grace was made perfect even in my weakness. When I was weak, that's when He was strong—*IN ME!*

So as I close this chapter, I am challenging you to do these five important things:

1. Take one last look back in amazement at the enemies that God has delivered you from.
2. Love your enemies. They are powerless against you!
3. Find your mark—It's *in you*!

4. Press forward!
5. Then rest *assured* with confidence as you obtain the promise!

"My goal is that they may be encouraged in heart and united in love, so that they may have the full riches of complete understanding, in order that they may know the mystery of God, namely, Christ." Colossians 2:2 NIV

His Workmanship & an Expensive Guarantee

God does not want a mere fraction of you. He wants *all* of you. He not only desires a portion of your worship. He wants you to worship Him *exclusively*. God not only seeks a part of our hearts, but desires that we love Him with our *whole* heart. Most of us at some point or another have experienced seasons of lack and seasons of plenty. And it is during the season of lack where we promise God our all.

We give Him all of our attention, our worship, and our tears—because we need to see His favor demonstrated on our behalf. We need to see things change. But far too often, once we obtain the blessing, once He gets us to a place we couldn't get to on our own—we have a tendency to slowly pull away from God. God is calling us to come closer to Him. Many times we enter stormy seasons, simply because He is calling us into a deeper relationship with Him. Is it only during our seasons of darkness and pain that we genuinely cry out to Him in love and adoration? Will He ever know us intimately, outside of our *distress*?

Is it only during these times of rejection and neglect that we remember how good *His* love feels? Is it only during our times of distress that God gets to hear the sound of His name called out? Why is it that when things appear to be going well and the sun is shining that God cannot hear our voices? He cannot hear His name being called out when our refrigerators are full, the gas tank is not empty, and the bills are paid. But why?

In the book of Matthew 6:33, Jesus tells us to *"seek ye first the Kingdom of God and His righteousness and all these things will be added unto you."* This is not just a mere magical scripture we use to get what we want from God—like a shiny ATM machine. It would be selfish of us to think this scripture were just about us. But that scripture reveals the desire God has for us to come after Him.

> And thou shalt love the Lord, thy God with all thine heart, and with all thy soul, and with all thy might.
> Deuteronomy 6:5 KJV

As a woman, I know what it is like to have the inner craving of being desired by a man. You want to know that he thinks enough of you to call you on the telephone to make and spend time with you. You want to know what it feels like when he creates an atmosphere for you and him to fellowship. You crave the feeling of being *pursued*. I'm a traditional woman—there is a special feeling that comes from hearing a man ask, "May I take you out for dinner?"

My life was greatly impacted by my great grandmother Zennie Mae down in Pine Mountain Georgia, my great aunt Amy Ray over in Decatur's East Lake Meadows high rise, and my grandfather Herman who was a Baptist preacher on the west side of Atlanta. They each taught me in their own respective ways, "Kim, don't you go chasing after boys. Let them come after you."

Sometimes, it could get frustrating and you would get tired of waiting. So you might find yourself as a young woman saying, "Let me just call him. Maybe I should just nudge him in my direction." But eventually, you learn that if you chased him and caught him, you would have to continue to *chase* him to *keep* him. But in essence, what you will ultimately discover is that what you have done is devalued yourself. Likewise when we chase after the things, we devalue God. *Hmmm…*

I was raised to be the type of woman that says, "Forget about the skin you see on the outside and come after ME. The Kimberly on the inside is much more valuable. She's much more interesting. Come after me. Show me that you are thinking about me. Show me that I am a *priority* to you".

God feels the same way. He wants to feel desired, He wants to be pursued. What He is saying in Matthew 6:33 is this: *"If you would just forget the tangible stuff that comes from being with me, and just come after ME, the stuff would lose its value."* God is saying, *"I can give you the stuff, that's no problem. But do you truly love ME? Do you value ME?"* In this scripture God is asking, *"Am I a priority to you?"*

There is no greater feeling than a feeling of value. And God is no different. God wants us to value Him. But what is value? Nothing can be compared to the relationship I have with the Father. Not a friendship, or relationship, not a job or car, and definitely not money or awards. Nothing could even come close to the value of my relationship with Him.

I am not afraid to admit that over the course of my life I have placed some people and many things in the wrong capacity. I have mistakenly given people and things more value than I should have. But each time, those people or things would fail to meet the high demands of what I should have only expected God to meet. Demands like: love, acceptance, affirmation, loyalty. I found out the hard way that only God can consistently give me these things without fail.

> *For we are His workmanship, created in Christ Jesus unto good works, which God hath before ordained that we should walk in them.*
> **Ephesians 2:10 KJV**

God values us so much that He considers us His workmanship. *[3]Marvin Sapp said it best when he sang, *"He saw the best in me, when everyone else around could only see the worst in me"*. No matter what everyone else sees, God sees you at your best. Even when you are down and out, He sees you as beautiful; something of great value.

When you walk onto a new home construction site, it's normally dirty, nasty, and trash is everywhere. If you didn't know any better you might drive up and say no don't stop here, keep going this place is filthy. But the builder doesn't see the trash. As a matter of fact the architect, who drew up the design and blueprint for the mansion does not walk up and see the trash. The architect knows the value of the materials lying around. He has the blueprint memorized in his mind, and instead of seeing dirt and trash- he sees a million dollar home. He sees chandeliers and wrap around porches. He sees whitewashed driveways and azalea bushes. He sees a masterpiece in the making.

When everyone else looks at you and can only see the mess in your life, or the mess you have come through—*God* sees the value in your materials. Your materials are the things used to make you who you are. The rape, the sickness, the cancer, the aids, the divorce, the inadequacies- those are your materials. They are not just piles of junk lying around. These are precious resources God uses to carefully craft you into the powerhouse you are!! My clothes may not be the latest fashion. My hair may not be neat and in perfect place. My shoes may be dirty and a little worn. But look a little deeper beneath the surface. I am *His* workmanship.

God looks at you and sees beyond the mess. He sees the finished product. He looks and sees something valuable and worth more than the stuff you have been through. And I would be remised if I didn't remind you that since you are made in His image, when He looks at you, He sees Himself! When you get up and look in the mirror you see a reflection of yourself, and if you get spiritual enough you will see God. Have you ever thought about the fact that you are actually God's mirror? Before He created man, He had no reflection.

> *I will praise thee; for I am fearfully and wonderfully made: marvelous are thy works; and that my soul knoweth right well.*
> **Psalm 139:14**

Now, when He wants to see a reflection of Himself He looks at you. That's why He will never leave you nor forsake you. God cannot leave Himself. That's why He is no respecter of persons. We are all a reflection of Him and if He denied any one of us, He'd be denying Himself! As long as we are placing the value on Him, making Him the priority, and chasing after *Him*....we are constantly increasing in value ourselves!!

When God considered us His workmanship, He was willing to put His name on it. He made us and sealed us with a guarantee. Consider this, when a Mercedes Benz is manufactured, it is *fearfully* and *wonderfully* made. Because it is classified as a Mercedes and carries the name Mercedes, it has to come with a certain guarantee. When you go to purchase a Mercedes, they provide you with a care package. Included in this care package is a list of all the warranties and guarantees that come along with its ownership.

Along with the care package you are provided with an owner's manual. The manual provides you with all the necessary instructions on how to take care of it. What kind of gasoline and oil to put in it to make it perform according to its greatest potential. Do you realize that you can be operating at less than your greatest potential if you are putting the wrong things in your life?

And then even after they have provided you with a care package, and provided you with the owners' manual, you are provided with a lifeline. Mercedes provides a 24-hr customer service call center to assist you in the event of an unforeseen emergency. Right above the sun visor, you will find an exclusive 1-800# printed for you to call in the event that you have a flat, run out of gas, or just breakdown anywhere. A Mercedes certified service technician will come to you, wherever you are and either repair it or take it to the dealership, while getting you to safety. And this is for the entire life of the car. You don't have to purchase a Triple *AAA* plan. They believe so much in the workmanship of their product that they can guarantee its maximum performance or they will come and pick it up.

What Mercedes Benz is saying is this, "As long as you do all the things we tell you to maintain this car it will operate at maximum performance. But even if something goes wrong, which we don't expect it to, we are willing to come where ever it is and fix it or pick it up for the entire life of this vehicle."

This is why you will hardly ever see a Mercedes Benz broken down on the side of the road. They consider their workmanship and their name to be so valuable, that they will not allow a negative perception to be created by having broken down cars on the side of the road for passersby to see.

I quickly learned that the guarantee that comes along with a Mercedes is much better than the guarantee of a Toyota, or a Nissan. Why is it better?

The Germans are comfortable offering a better care package because of their *workmanship*. The Germans guarantee that they have not cut any corners. They guarantee that they have used the best of every part—screws, nuts, and bolts—to manufacture this car.

Contrarily, other manufacturers don't offer such an attractive warranty because of their workmanship. They know that at some point this car is going to wear out and they are not willing to be held liable for the cost of repairing it. Instead they want you to just buy another car.

Like the Mercedes Benz, you are God's best workmanship and you come with an expensive lifetime guarantee! When God considered us His workmanship, He was willing to put His name on it. He made us and then sealed us with a guarantee through the blood of Jesus Christ. He gave us a care package for this vessel we are operating. He guarantees us that He made us with the best of everything mind, body, and soul. You were fearfully and wonderfully made!

Now if we put junk in our lives, we will not operate at maximum capacity. We will just putter along the way barely surviving. Always tired and never reaching the fullest potential God created us to perform in. But if we maintain this vessel the way He instructed us to, we will wow the observers. If we use it to chase after Him and make Him the priority, we will operate at maximum capacity. If we maintain this vessel the way He instructed us to, we will *wow* those who are watching us pass by.

Now here is the *warranty*. He tells us that even if something goes down with this vessel after doing all that He has told us to do. He will send a service tech, (a.k.a. the Holy Spirit) to either repair the problem on the spot, or take us back to the manufacturer (God) to be restored.

I was driving my Mercedes C-Class a few years ago and hit a speed breaker in the parking lot. It totally blew my tire. Another time I got a nail in the tire. Both times they came out and totally restored the tire. Now, these were both issues that I caused. But the Mercedes manufacturer knew about something called grace! They said to me, we are still willing to fix the problem because it's still our workmanship! God says, "Even if you do something to cause this vessel I created you in to malfunction, I have enough grace for you that I will send the Holy Ghost to repair the problem. No matter where you go wrong you are still *MY* workmanship".

On your feet now—applaud God! Bring a gift of laughter, sing yourselves into his presence. Know this: God is God, and God, God. He made us; we didn't make him. We're his people, his well-tended sheep. Enter with the password: "Thank you!" Make yourselves at home, talking praise. Thank him. Worship him. For God is sheer beauty, all-generous in love, loyal always and ever.

(Psalm 100 The MSG Bible)

9

Our Faith—His Will

Everything you see is subject to change; first in the spiritual realm and then in the natural realm. Hebrews 11:1, the most famous faith scripture recited easily by most of us, begins with 3 very important but undervalued words: *Now faith is*. These 3 words are very small in size, but very significant in value.

Now, indicates that we are speaking of a present moment in time. When you use the term now in any instance you are absolutely positively referring to the present static moment; a moment that will only exist at this particular and specific time. A moment that once it's gone, you will never retrieve it, repeat it, or relive it again.

Faith, indicates that no matter what you see or don't see in the natural, something on the inside of you must imagine, and then believe in the possibility of something else. Faith indicates that there is a belief so strong in the invisible and the intangible that it has become a confident assurance. Not a guess, a possibility, or an idea of something to manifest. But it is an assurance. And if faith equals the evidence, the fact that you have faith, means that you have *IT*; whatever *IT* is!

Is, becomes the ammunition that catapults faith into its peak of performance. *Is* defines the current state of Faith. *Is*, defies "becoming" and stands alone in "already". Faith is not becoming the evidence, but it already *is*. Not *trying to be*, not *will be*, not *shall be*, but simply *IS*.

By reading this verse in the message bible we understand a lot more about the scripture that has become almost cliché with the christian experience.

The fundamental fact of existence is that this trust in God, this Faith, is the firm foundation under everything that makes life worth living. It's our handle on what we can't see.
Hebrews 11:1 MSG Bible

Simply put, *faith* is our handle on what we cannot see. And once we have grasped the handle of faith with a firm grip and refuse to let go—then no matter what we see, the thing, the idea, the dream—that we hold onto by faith, must eventually manifest. That means everything you can see with your eyes, must respond and transform in accordance with the transformation that has occurred within you. When a supernatural change takes place in the spirit–what you see around you has no choice but to be aligned with that transformation.

> *Truly I tell you, whatever you bind (deny) on earth will be bound (denied) in heaven, and whatever you loose (embrace) on earth will be loosed (embraced) in heaven*
>
> *Psalm 139:14 NKJV emphasis mine*

Now don't take this and run in any direction with the idea that whatever "you want" you can have just because there is a "want". What's most important about the whole faith message is that whatever you have faith for must line up with God's will. That's right! In order for you to obtain a promise fulfilled by God, it must also be *His* promise.

Do you understand that before you can *see* a thing, you must *see* a thing?? The Lord says, "Whatever you deny or reject in my presence through prayer, I will deny its access in your life on the Earth. And likewise, whatever you embrace or receive in my presence through prayer, I will release it into your life on earth." And that is the spiritual definition of synchronicity.

Over time, I have always been amazed at the study of synchronicity. When you take the time to understand the power of your personal prayers and thoughts, as a result you will become more conscious of what you allow your lives and your actions to become synchronized with.

It is important that we learn the importance of not imitating that which we see in the natural—because what we see is temporary. But instead, we should imitate that which we see in the spirit—because what we can't see is eternal.

The word *"synchronize"* means to make something happen at the same time. The word *synchronicity* means that the movement of one thing is aligned and perfectly parallel to the movement of another.

One of my favorite Olympic events, outside of the track and field events, is synchronized diving. Every 4 years after I watch the opening ceremonies, I always check to see what night the synchronized diving event is aired. I am always amazed as I sit there on my sofa and watch the divers stand poised on the tip of the diving board and prepare to plunge to the depths below. They stand there at the edge of the board, take a moment and bring their bodies and breathing patterns into total submission and alignment—one to another. First, they make sure neither of their bodies are moving. Then they make sure they are both relaxed and breathing at the same pace.

Once they are both quieted and stilled, they then begin to plunge into the water at the same speed and making the same moves—at the exact same time. Sometimes the synchronicity is off and one may land too soon. One may even make a move too late. But in synchronized diving every move made out of line is seen by the judges and the world at large. They will even replay the errors and slow the playback down so we can all study and scoff at the move that went wrong. Sounds a lot like life right?

In 2012, something amazing happened during the women's synchronized diving event. It had been 12 years since the US team had won a medal in the diving events. None of the teams in 2008, or 2004 were able to line themselves up closely enough to be considered completely synchronized. Something was always just a little too –*off*. For 12 years they were out of sync.

But this year, the world witnessed America dust off the ashes of defeat and rise to the podium to claim her award. I watched as the two divers, went to the diving board for several rounds mastering a perfectly aligned dive each time. Then I watched the crowd's anticipation grow as they took the diving board one last time. This final dive would determine the fate of the US diving status for another 4 years. After taking a deep breath and saying "let's go with it!" they both plunged in to the water.

The results? Kelci Bryant, and Abigail Johnston scored a 321.90 to win the first ever medal in this event for the Americans. This time, after 12 years of being 'out of sync', the US wins the silver medal. After 12 years of being out of alignment the USA finally obtained the victory!

Then something happened that made it all connect for me. I watched the girls walk away from the water excited and happy as their friends, coaches, and family cheered in happiness for the victory. I saw one of the girls walk over to the side alone. In amazement, *she began to jump, she cried, she wept in victory.*

I believe that there was a personal moment of gratitude to something much higher than herself. She knew that it was not her alone who had perfected the dive. She knew that she could not have succeeded in her own strength. She had faith in something greater than her own ability. As she fell forward on her knees in tears I began to weep with her. In that moment I shared her emotion.

Watching her rejoice caused me to reflect on the fact that I too, after many years of rebellion, have finally come into sync with the Father. For many years I had been out of order; out of alignment with Him. For 12 years, I like the diver, just couldn't seem to sync up with God. I love Him and I know He loves me. He has kept me as I have worked feverishly to succeed. But the things in my life just kept going *wrong*. Things God wanted from me, I refused to give Him. People He wanted me to release, I held on to for dear life. Choices He wanted me to make, I spitefully deviated from His plan. Routes He wanted me to travel in order to learn something inspirational for my life, I'd always look for a shortcut. But in 2012, I finally got it right with God. Finally in 2012 I had grown to appreciate being in sync with what God has for my life. And like the diver, I have found myself in a place of rejoicing, weeping, and worship. My heart and mind is clear. I can freely let go of the people and things that don't line up with His plan for my life. I can freely move according to His footsteps. I am no longer trying to drive. I am at a place I never thought I would get to. There is nothing like being FREE!!

It was then that I learned, the key to being synchronized to God is being in the *NOW*- being in His present glory. When you are not focused on yesterday and are instead faced toward Him we can move forward as He moves.

Can you remember what it was like as a child to go up to your Father and lay your head on his chest and listen to His heartbeat? I never had that experience, but I learned over time that when we are on our knees in prayer, we are really placing our head against the Father's heart. When we are on our knees in prayer, and we come to a still and quiet place of worship—we can hear the heartbeat of the Father. And then, when we hear His heartbeat—we can hear His plans for us.

The greatest tragedy of life is to spend it traveling in one direction, only to find out at the end that we were supposed to be traveling the opposite way. When it's too late, you cannot turn back. You get frustrated because you realize you don't have enough time left to correct the mistakes.

We can love, pray for, and chase people and things our entire lives only to find out that it wasn't God's plan for us. Most times we find that if we had only waited and searched deeper in God, the blessings He had in store for us, were much greater than the ones we chose for ourselves. Most times, the paths *we* choose will lead us down a path that does not even remotely resemble with the path *He* carved out for us. Our chosen paths can sometimes cause us to end up way over *here* when God intended for us to be way over *there*.

> *For everything in the world—the lust of the flesh, the lust of the eyes, and the pride of life—comes not from the Father but from the world.*
> *1 John 2:16 NKJV*

But we get distracted and derailed by 3 most obvious enemies: *the lust of the eye, lust of the flesh, and the pride of life*. We overspend because things look good on the shelf or because we want the attention that comes from having it. We do things and get in relationships that stroke our egos and make us feel good. And finally many of us have developed prideful attitudes to which we think we don't need God.

But it is impossible to please God without faith! It is impossible to go deeper with God without faith. It is impossible to obtain the abundant life God intended for you without faith. The thing you desire most, may look attractive at the moment, it might be the popular thing to do…

But is it God's will for your life??

Choosing to surrender our will to His, most times will cost you heartbreak, abandonment, and isolation. People will not understand your decision to do things God's way. But I encourage you to stay the course with Him and move according His plan. In the end those that left you for dead will have to ask, "*WHO* is this God that you serve??"

And those that don't know Him will be won over by the power of your testimony. We each have a responsibility to bring somebody else into the kingdom. But they cannot be won when you testi-*LIE*!!! You must have your proof. Like the disciple Thomas, they will say, "Show me the hole in your side. Show me where they nailed you in your hands; show me the scars you walked away with." In other words, people who don't know the power and impact of a life with Jesus will say, "Show me your stripes! Show me the proof and the evidence that you actually went through something and lived to tell the story. Tell me how you have suffered. Show me the wounds first—then tell me the story!"

When we come into alignment with God, our prayers are more effective. We are constantly in prayer asking God to do something for us. We were told to be specific in our prayers right? But, how often do you pray and ask God, "Will you show me your plan?"

Yes! The bible does tell us to, "be anxious for nothing and by prayer and supplication present your requests to God". (Phil. 4:6-7) Yes! The bible tells us to, "delight ourselves in the Lord and He will give us the desires of our heart". (Ps.37:4) Yes! The bible tells us that it is "His pleasure to bless us". (Lk.12:32) However, the bible also reminds us that, "God is a rewarder of them that diligently *seek HIM.*" *(Heb.11:6)* We must be so careful to seek His *way*, seek His *plan*, and seek His *heart*. The blessings and miracles God has in store for us, are many times locked up, *IN-STORE*, because we are praying and believing for the wrong thing. It is important to understand that when we pray –we must pray His will!

When we pray the Lord's prayer we end with, "Let Thy Kingdom come and Thy will be done" *right*???

Finally, once we begin to pray His will, it is only then that we can begin to tap into the "Now Faith Is." When we pray His will, we are unlocking the supernatural power of God to be seen in our lives. Doors begin to swing open that we could not have opened ourselves. We begin to find ourselves in the right place at the right time, on schedule for our divine appointments.

I will be the first to confess that there was a time when I prayed *"make this man be the one"*, or *"make this interview be successful."* But each time I prayed those prayers, I instantly tied God's hands. I was in fact saying, "NO" to His best for me. And as a result, I embraced and granted access to whatever hell and drama that came along with my backwards prayers.

God is God alone—and He doesn't need our help. For many of us, God is waiting for our prayers to change so that they line up with His plan. There is so much that God wants to do in our lives. But, He loves us so much that He gave us the gift to choose.

In Genesis, God said, "Let us make man in our image and according to our likeness, let them have dominion". (Gen.1:26) Deuteronomy reads, "I have set before you today *life* and *death*, But I pray you choose life!" (Duet. 30:19) I put these two scriptures together to say this: since God gave you dominion, He will not do what you don't invite Him to do.

I spent 12 years of my life, trying to do things my way, I chose the husband I wanted, I bought the house I wanted, I opened the business that I wanted. I bought the cars I wanted. But after going through turmoil while in it, I eventually prayed and begged God take it all away—the house, the cars, the job, and the bad relationships. My prayer became, "LORD, start me over again, do it your way!! I am a clean and empty canvas. God paint the picture you want to see." And after I got over the fear of letting go, like jumping out of a plane, I dove head first into His hands.

As a result, I got the dream job I had only imagined having. He gave me the best car I had ever driven. He cleaned up my relationships. He renewed my self-esteem. And most of all, I wake up each day rejoicing, and in awe at what it feels like to be in sync with Him.

10

But What I Do Have, I Give It...

I am going to challenge each of you reading this book to re-adjust the attitude you take when you give. It does not matter if you have ever served another human being, be it through your local church, community outreach center, or maybe someone in your family just needed help with an electric bill. Far too often, we limit our giving capacity by mistakenly resting on the idea that the recipient only needed financial assistance. We assume the homeless community is in dire need of money, when really they are dying inside because they have lived their entire lives being *mis*-understood. We assume they need shelter, when really what they are hungry for is inspiration. In the winter months we minimize their dry skin and cold hands as a need for warm gloves and a new sweater; ignoring the fact they have spent one to many winters lacking an experience in the atmosphere of warm authentic love. It's time to readjust our giving attitude.

Let's read ACTS 3:1-10 (NIV):

> One day Peter and John were going up to the temple at the time of prayer— at three in the afternoon. 2 Now a man who was lame from birth was being carried to the temple gate called Beautiful, where he was put every day to

beg from those going into the temple courts. 3 When he saw Peter and John about to enter, he asked them for money. 4 Peter looked straight at him, as did John. Then Peter said, "Look at us!" 5 So the man gave them his attention, expecting to get something from them.

6 Then Peter said, "Silver or gold I do not have, but what I do have I give you. In the name of Jesus Christ of Nazareth, walk." 7 Taking him by the right hand, he helped him up, and instantly the man's feet and ankles became strong. 8 He jumped to his feet and began to walk. Then he went with them into the temple courts, walking and jumping, and praising God. 9 When all the people saw him walking and praising God, 10 they recognized him as the same man who used to sit begging at the temple gate called Beautiful, and they were filled with wonder and amazement at what had happened to him.

It is important that we identify with Peter's *confession* (which demonstrates his faith), Peter's *loving* (which demonstrates how we should love), and Peter's *gift of Hope* (which demonstrates Peter's ability to properly assess *what* he needed to give).

> Now the Purpose of the commandment is love from a pure heart, from a good conscience, and from sincere faith
> 1Tim.1:5 NKJV

Peter's Confession. As we observe Peter's development, we discover that even though at one very low point of weakness he denied the Savior, he was also a man of great faith. But it was in that low weak state that his faith was unveiled. Like many of us, Peter did not have a clue to just how faithful he would be. He had no idea until he had been challenged in a very dangerously confusing situation to muster up the courage to look beyond his limitations and exercise the faith to overcome the greatest giant in his life—*FEAR*.

"Peter do you love me?" Jesus asked him 3 times. And each time He replied, "Yes." Peter replied yes from a pure heart. Of course we know that the Lord does not ask a question that he does not already know the answer to. He warned Peter that Satan desired to *"sift him as wheat"* and that he would eventually deny him 3 times.

But in essence what the Lord was saying to Peter was, "Look I know you love me, but the enemy is going to cause you to stumble. And because I know your love is sincere, I have already prayed for you; so when you give up and throw in the towel in your human nature, your *faith* would not fail you." Jesus goes on to inspire Peter by saying, "And when you come through (when you wake up and realize just how strong you really are) you will then be anointed to set the others free." (Lk. 22:31-33)

Jesus wanted Peter and (you as well) to know that once you find out who you really are, and whose you are, and what you are made of, you can really do some damage to the devil. There is nothing you can't do!! Jesus was preparing Peter to be delivered from the fear that controlled his life—so that he could return and set others free.

So let's reverse and go back for a minute.

- ❖ In the Old Testament: Moses said, "Who will I tell them has sent me?" God said, "I am that I am."
- ❖ In the New Testament: Jesus asked Peter, "*Peter* who do you say that I am?"
- ❖ Several times in the New Testament Jesus used Peter to teach us lessons on faith and love.
- ❖ 1John 4:18 states that "Perfect love (God's love) casts out all fear".

How many of you know that it is utterly impossible to both have faith and also be afraid at the same time? So if you have *perfect love*, you can have faith—because fear is cast out. That's why *nothing* shall separate me from the love of GOD!!! When the disciples were afraid of who Jesus might be, Peter in Faith, replied to Jesus, "You are the Christ". Because He *loved* Him, He *believed* in Him.

Hebrews 11:6 tells us, "They that come to the Father must believe that He is, and that He is a rewarder of them that diligently seek Him". When Jesus told Peter to walk out towards him on the water, in the storm, He wanted Peter to learn that, "I love you too much to let you drown. I love you too much to allow you to be swept away in the storm. So you can have faith in that!"

When we fall into various situations, if we would just remember *His love* for us, we can be confident that we will come out on top...*everytime*! It takes faith to love; and it takes love to give.

Peter's Gift of Hope. In Acts 3:6, Peter spoke to the man (we don't know his name) who had spent his days begging for handouts, whatever others could spare, to help him make ends meet. He positioned himself in a place where he knew people were armed with money, going into the temple. If you were in a position of need, of course you would go to a place where you absolutely knew people could help you, *right? So we can understand the man's position.* But how many of us are in a place of need right now? Everybody, right?

Everybody reading this book is in a position of needing *something* right now. My need might not be your need. Your need might not be your neighbor's need. But everybody needs something. I'm going to go so far as to say that the greatest need of every person reading this book is love. Now you might be saying, "Oh I already have love", or "I'm good, I don't need love at all." But I am not convinced that there is a single reader who does not wake up each day looking for a touch, or a smile, understanding, a listening ear, or a simple act of kindness. No one is exempt from the need of love. I am willing to go so far as to say the man who lay at the gate, was not just looking for alms or money, he had only grown accustomed to that because that's what people thought he needed. Or that's all people were willing to give. Nobody was willing to look deeper. How many of you just wish people would look deeper when they look at you? People may come in and out of your lives, just passing through, not willing to stop and spend real time with you to look deeper into your heart and spirit to understand your position.

But when Peter and John came along, they didn't respond like everyone else did. They didn't give what everyone else gave. They stopped, looked deeper, got his attention, and gave him his heart's desire: LOVE. They loved him enough to challenge him to change his position! See someone can give you money, but money does not always change your position. I can get money to buy me a two piece snack today, but my position has not changed. My mind has not changed. My perspective on the things I have experienced has not changed.

> For God so loved the world that He gave his only begotten Son, that whoever believes in Him should not perish, but have everlasting life.
>
> John 3:16 NKJV

Look at that! For God so loved that He did what? He GAVE!! He loved. Therefore, He *gave*. Loving = Giving. If you are not *giving*, then you are not *loving*. So if you say you are *loving*, then tell me how you are *giving*. When God demonstrated His love for us, His giving changed our position!

A lot of times we go into relationships looking for what we can get from the relationship. I think we have all done it at some time or another. But we go in with the question, "What is this person investing in my life? What does this person have that may increase the quality of my life?" And sadly, we end relationships prematurely because we don't think we are gaining anything from it.

The challenge is changing our perspective of one another's contribution in relationships. You might have to begin to ask yourself, "Even though they didn't give me what I asked for, is it possible that they gave me something of greater value, something intangible? Did I grow in any way in this relationship?"

Let's talk about God's contribution. God loved us so much that He gave. But just because He loves us does not mean that He gives us everything we ask and pray for. Instead, He challenges us to seek His best for us. I know that's always a tough reality to accept. But if I can just get you to reflect back for a moment, about all the times you prayed, cried, and begged for something, yet God's hand did not appear to move for things to turn out in favor of your request. Then days, weeks, or months later you find out why you didn't get what appeared to be the blessing. You may have even discovered that it would have been the biggest mistake you ever made. Consequently, you thanked God that He did not answer your prayer and in essence saved you from yourself.

See, the man lying at the gate, was accustomed to asking for money, but Peter didn't give him that. Peter recognized that money was not what he *really* needed. Peter loved him too much to enable his handicap. He loved him enough to give him what he needed - *HOPE!*

> And Now these three remain: faith hope, and love. But the greatest of these is love.
>
> John 3:16 NIV

In some versions of scripture, *love* is instead written as *charity*. And of course, charity is a means to express a capacity to give. So I repeat: We are not *loving*, if we are not *giving*.

And finally we get to identify how God used Peter to demonstrate His love. Jesus told Peter, "If you love me feed my sheep". In my own humble definition, feeding is an act of nourishing another that does not have the capacity or the know how to nourish *itself*. Feeding is an act of giving, which comes from a heart of loving. When you can look beyond your own emotional, spiritual, and physical needs, when you can see beyond growling stomachs and empty pantries, it is then that God is ready to use you. Your need may be very important and you may need a 'right now' blessing from God. Your husband may be threatening to walk out, the college tuition for your child is due, and they are threatening layoffs on your job. But it is at that very moment instead that God will cause you to reach out to fill someone else's empty purse and minister to their broken heart. It is then that God has challenged you to demonstrate the faith He has already given to you and begin to give from a pure heart.

Who are the sheep? The sheep are God's people. What is Peter feeding the sheep? As we can see from Peter's demonstration, he fed God's people love. LOVE!! The very thing that Jesus asked him about 3 times was the very thing God used to build Peter's ministry. If we go back to the gate called Beautiful, he didn't feed the man food. Nor did he give him money for food, He fed him *love*. Love changed his position. So now, being in a new position in his heart and in his mind, he can begin to discipline himself, grow up and, and get his own food!

Most of you reading this book don't need money. You don't need money any more than I do. You need for someone to come into your life and challenge you to change your thinking. That is *love*! Peter cut off the ear of the Roman soldier because he was in a position of loving and giving. Peter could have been arrested, beaten, or killed at that moment. He loved Jesus so much that he was willing, at this moment, to give his life for him. But God does not call us to *give* our lives for him in *love*. He has already given the only life which was worthy to be given. But He does call us to *live* our lives for Him. He calls us to live our lives in such a way that others who do not know Him may experience Him through our capacity to *love*.

Paul tells us in Colossians:

> Therefore, as the elect of God, holy and beloved, put on tender mercies, kindness, humility, meekness, longsuffering; bearing with one another, and forgiving one another, if anyone has a complaint against another; even as Christ forgave you, so you also must do. But above all these things put on love, which is the bond of perfection. And let the peace of God rule in your hearts, to which also you were called in one body; and be thankful.
> Colossians 3:14 NKJV

11

Right Now — I AM

During the Christmas holiday season, people all over the world are excited, shopping, filled with the spirit of love and charity. Many are making elaborate preparations to close the year out with great celebrations. Though all the nostalgia grows around me, I can't help but to be sensitive to the reality of the tragedies that seem to increase around the holiday season.

Each year on my birthday, I always make it a point to be awake when the clock strikes midnight. And each year I experience a mixture of emotions. Each year I find myself growing more excited and grateful for being blessed with something as precious as life. You can't put a price on it. You can't wrap it up in fancy wrapping paper. You can't party hard enough to express the value of this one intangible gift. I am noticing that the older I get, and the more tragedies I witness around me, I become more and more grateful for every day and year that I can say, "I am still here!" I find myself in awe and growing in gratitude that I am simply "alive".

Life is beautiful, but it is also very fragile—we should always handle it with care. No task to be completed or accomplishment to be fulfilled could compare to the simple idea of existence. We run through life from one phase to the next trying to become something greater than before. We go through school, college, and pursue marriages, divorces, careers and wealth to have it all left behind us once we transition into eternity. We spend most of our lives peering through foggy eyes trying to figure out which way to go. But the older we get the clearer the picture becomes. The older we get and the closer we get to the grave, we discover through all of the rushing, pursuing, and trying to become—we have failed to just BE. I am not afraid of dying—but I am afraid of dying without having tasted the real abundance of *life*.

So it is important that we learn to just be in the current moment and enjoy life. I am not suggesting that we cast off restraint and live a life without discipline or direction. But each time we take a single deep breath, it is important that we pursue the *right now*.

- ❖ Pursue the Right Now God—We serve a God who is always present with us! He is a very present help in the time of trouble. Here is there with you right now. (Psalm 46:1)

- ❖ Pursue the Right Now Faith—Now faith is!! (Hebrews 11:1)

- ❖ Pursue the Right Now Mercy—His mercy endures forever, its new every morning, there is <u>NOW</u> therefore no condemnation to those who are in Christ Jesus (Romans 8:1) You don't have to wait and fast to be forgiven. You are forgiven before you even miss the mark!

- ❖ Pursue the Right Now Grace—His grace is sufficient for me *in the midst* of my weakness. You don't have to wait and pray for God to *give you* the strength to press through your situation. You already have it. (2 Corinthians 12:9)

- ❖ Pursue the Right Now Love—Nothing can ever separate us from the love of God. Not bills, not my failures, not my enemies. When nothing else could help me *love lifted me*! You don't have to sit around and wait on a soulmate to know authentic love. God's love is available to you right now. (Romans 8:39)

- ❖ Pursue the Right Now Favor—That door that you are waiting to be opened to you, is already open! God has already decided that blessings will overtake you. Surely, goodness and mercy shall follow you all the days of your life! (Psalm 23:6)

- ❖ <u>Pursue the Right Now Joy</u>—I don't have to wait until all the bills have been paid and my teenagers are out of the house to be happy. In the presence of the Lord is the fullness of joy. (Psalm 16:11)

- ❖ <u>Pursue the Right Now Peace</u>— We don't have to wait until the problem is resolved. Knowing that God sees the end from the beginning, and that He has already provided a way of escape—I can have the peace that surpasses all understanding. When others think I *should* be losing my mind—they will look at my composure and wonder *"Why are you so calm?"* (Philippians 4:7)

> Praise the Lord Oh my soul, and forget not ALL His benefits.
>
> Psalm 103:2

When Moses inquired of the Lord, "Who shall I tell them has sent me?" He said, "Tell them, *I am* sent you." Notice God didn't say *I will be*, or *I was*. He said, "I am". So right now, you may as well go ahead and shout it out loud, "Right Now, I AM!"

"Am" is the present participle of the verb "being". So in essence, God was referring to Himself as an always present being. He said tell them, "the Force that is always present and forever with me has also sent me." He said "Tell them a Force greater than mankind has not sent you, but actually brought you". He was making note of the fact that you are not merely being sent—you are being brought! You are not showing up alone. God is with you right now. God is with you tomorrow. He is with you when you show up at the doctor's office. He is with you when you show up to speak. He is with you when you show up in the court room. You weren't sent. But you were carried by the active force that does not answer to man!

So when God says, "I AM"—this tells us God is *always* in a state of *being*! This tells us He is always *with us*! That's why when the prophet Isaiah prophesied the coming of Christ, He said: "She will give birth to a son and will call him Immanuel (which means 'God is with us')." (Isaiah 7:14 NLT)

What is God doing right now? He is *being*. Well, since He is being—Then He is always operating in His element. What does that mean—*operating in His element*? We were all created with a unique state of *being*. I may be a talent manager in corporate America. And I may be successful in my role. But it requires a lot of study and work. My role requires a high level of resilience when leadership challenges arise. At times I have wanted to quit. But so that I didn't quit, I had to remind myself, "Kimberly you have a family—people are depending on you. No matter how much you want to quit—you must keep pushing." In order to push when I feel like giving up, I have to constantly rely on His grace to stay in position.

Now on the other hand, I am a minister of the Gospel. I am an author. I am a motivator. These are the things that I seem to do without any strenuous effort. The talent just appears to flow when I am operating in my gifting. So when I am doing these things—I don't ever think about quitting. I can operate in them fluently and sometimes in my sleep with no added stress or pressure.

When I am fully in my element, it is obvious to me (and to others) that this is the capacity I was created to function in. When I am allowed the creative freedom to use the gifts God gave me, my mind begins moving and working on things that bring fulfillment to my soul. Even when I am tired, I have to get up and write some things out.

Of all the years I volunteered at the homeless outreach center, it never felt like work. Instead, it always brought joy to my soul simply to arrive and encourage each of the guests from all walks of life, no matter what struggle or addiction they battled. Volunteering gave me life and it watered my soul to simply share the love of God without someone who needed a reminder.

I am sharing all of this to say, I have to give my mind an opportunity to create and do what it likes to do.

Walking in my God-given gift is nourishment for my mind. If I don't get the opportunity to operate in my gift, then my mind will begin to crave, then starve for an opportunity to release the force of God building on the inside of me. Slowly, over time I begin to die.

So when we say God is "in His Element" we are merely referring to God doing what He does best—*Be Himself*. He is *being Himself* when He is answering prayers, providing for our needs, opening doors for our dreams to come true, closing doors on our past failures, and bringing light in the darkest moments of our lives. He is *being Himself* when He is loving the unlovable, forgiving the unforgivable, and performing the impossible. He is *being Himself* when He is bringing life back into dead situations. These are the activities that bring Him fulfillment and joy. It delights Him when we step out of His way and let God BE *Himself*!!

> Beloved, I wish above all things that you may prosper and be in health, even as your soul prospers.
> 1 John 3:2 NKJV

It is God's desire that you would prosper and be in good health, even as your soul prospers. He enjoys being involved in your success. It pleases God to bring you joy. I don't know about you but if someone is saying it would please *them* to bless *me*—I don't see a reason to withhold from them an opportunity to be pleased. So I say, "By all means have your way GOD!"

Now when the great I AM is in His element, He can always hear you when you pray. He can always feel you when you hurt. He can always understand you when you are confused. There is never a time when He is an absent or deadbeat Father. God is never pretending or practicing. He is not a mad scientist. He is always right there. Since He is always in His state of BEING—He is always being Himself. So that's why when I pray, I like to say God just BE! God just be God! Just do what you do!

Because as long as He is in His state of *being*, then everything is *already alright*! As long as He is in His state of "I AM-*ness*", things are working for my good! Even during times when it appears everything is a mess in my life, once I think about the fact that *I AM* is on the throne, all worry and doubt comes to an end. *I AM* is in control —so I don't have to try and figure it out. *I AM* has already worked it out!!

Even as I am praying, when it hits my spirit that I am praying to the great *I AM*, I instantly advance to another level in my prayer. It becomes clear to me that the very thing that I am praying for and about—has already been resolved by *I AM*. Even as we are praying, He is *being* God!!! When we get up off our knees, we can expect to see the manifestation of His I AM-*ness*.

When my oldest son went away to visit his father for the weekend, I would immediately go into his room and do an inventory and clean things up my way. All moms will understand what I mean when I say, He has his way, and then I have *my* way. So if you walk into the room you can instantly tell who has been in there by the way we leave it. The way I clean has my *detailed* signature on it. His *half-way* cleaning is his signature.

Likewise, when I get up off my knees from praying—I can always tell by the way the atmosphere has changed around me that God has been in the room. When God has been in the room cleaning up the mess in ME— He leaves His signature. Things in my life just begin to fall in to place. My relationships are in order. My conversations are more peaceful. I am more productive and more patient on my job. I don't respond to drama and stress with anxiety. I can *always* tell when God has been in the room.

This is just a short commercial for somebody that needs to hear it. But when was the last time you took a break from the stuff in your life and just let God come in the room and do a work in you? When was the last time you allowed Him come in and clean things up His way?

It is encouraging to know that in the midst of your storm, in the midst of your uncertainty, we don't have to wait to search after God to give us an answer. His answers, His provision, and His healing, are all available to us **RIGHT NOW.**

> According as His divine power has given unto us all things that pertain unto life and godliness, through the knowledge of Him who has called us to glory and virtue
>
> 2Peter 1:3 NKJV

The bible tells me that, He has already given us everything we need for our journey in life. He has already blessed us with every spiritual blessing. Therefore, why continue through life with a mentality that tells me I have to wait for God to come and do what He has *already* done? It's time out for that. God said, "I AM!!" He already *IS*!! So what more are you waiting for Him to *do???*

The whole Earth is waiting for the sons of God, the mature church (which is you-not a physical building) to rise up and take their rightful place and their position of authority over the works of the enemy. (Rom.8:19) But you cannot rise up and take authority if you don't first recognize that you have it.

Jesus said, "Verily, verily, I say unto you, He that believeth on me, the works that I do shall he do also; and greater works than these shall he do; because I go unto my Father." (John 14:12) Jesus was able to operate in His full authority because he understood that God is *I AM*. And he recognized what power was already available in him, through *I AM*. So as soon as we get the mind which was also in Christ Jesus, then we will begin to see the greater works. It is time for the supernatural power of God to hit our lives. But you must believe in order for it to work in your life.

Dear readers, God is with us! And He is omnipotent. He is able to be everywhere at the same time. His omnipresence means that He can be here with me when I am volunteering at the outreach center, with my mother in her apartment, and with my aunt in the hospital; all at the same time! His omnipresence means He can be with your son in a jail cell and your sister in divorce court. He is with your brother while he is on chemotherapy and with you under a bridge—at the same time! Now I know we are all created in His image, but that is one characteristic we did not get. As much as our friends and family would like us to be, we cannot be everywhere at the same time.

There is no place that He is *not*... Because HE IS! Isn't that amazing? He is right now with you wherever you are in your journey—He has been with you all along. I know people get so caught up in the gifts, toys and company parties. But this is what the whole Christmas holiday season is about: *Immanuel*. It is our annual reminder that we are not alone in this galaxy. God is with us.

When Adam and Eve were cast out of Eden, they left with the misunderstanding that God was no longer with them. And when Cain went out and killed his brother Able, he had no idea that God was actually *with him*. But when Jesus was born, the message God was sending to the entire human race, was that "I am *still* with you". And then before Jesus died on the cross, God so eloquently spoke to us through the vocal chords of Christ. He made us an audible promise saying "I will never leave you nor forsake you; I'll be with you even until the end!" I'd like to think that was the secondary purpose of the coming of Christ. It was so simple. It was so that God could get an audible, visible, and tangible message to us that we could all hear, see, touch, and understand that "*I am still with you*!"

So as you move forward in your journey, do so with the understanding that you don't have to wait for something to *"happen"* in order to walk into your destiny. You don't have to wait for your calling to be revealed. You already have everything you need to complete the work He created you to do. I AM is on the throne. He is operating in His element. He is available to you *RIGHT NOW!*

12

Finding Your Place, While In the Process

It can be so very difficult to determine who you are and what you are supposed to be doing with your life. I have known people very close to me to struggle with the fear and frustration that time may be running out for them. They feel that they have spent most of their lives seeking purpose without any success and that time may be running out for them to have signified their reason for existence.

My challenge for you today is: find your place while you are still in the process. Finding your "place" while still dealing with your day-to-day tasks and responsibilities requires a lot of patience, waiting, and focus. As the saying goes, "Rome was not built in single day", the broken pieces of your heart and the shattered dreams about your life, will not be restored in a single day.

Being healed and restored requires that you take a deep breath, crawl, then walk, and then begin to run through the process. Finding your place is about divorcing yourself from the painful memories and failed attempts to succeed. Therefore, it is ultimately about discovering and embracing your divine assignments.

This chapter is for those who know they are on their way somewhere, but are many times frustrated with the day to day objections. You know the inconvenient problems that arise, and the people that you talk to that might suggest to you that, *"this is all there is"*. There are times when you know without a doubt that you heard the voice of God concerning you. But there is always that one person who will object to the will of God for your life. You know, the person who can never really see clearly on how to work out their own mess, but as you continue to grow and prosper they can *always* somehow figure out how to resolve your problems—*right*??

As you are on your way to the promise, God would have me to inform you that there is an assignment for you, while in the process. The assignment is not intended to frustrate, disappoint, or discourage you. But the assignment is intended to prepare and strengthen you for where you are headed. The assignment is designed to foster your personal growth. There are some habits, ideas, and attitudes that just don't line up with where you are going. Therefore, God has to change your mind.

The assignment is also intended to weed out the people who don't deserve to be on the front row of your life's performance. It is time for you to you begin to identify who even deserves a ticket at all. Some folks were assigned to distract you and work against you. Some folk were assigned to just work your last nerve. These folk belong up on the balcony! And then there are some folk whose only agenda is to assassinate you. These folk don't deserve a ticket at all!

Now, God could just escort them out of your life Himself. But the assignment is designed to help you see people for who they are and be so fed up with hanging around the wrong people that you cut them off on your own.

See if you get to the point where you are forced to break off dysfunctional relationships on your own, then chances are you won't disobey God and reopen those doors again. God is not going to remove people *forcefully* from your life. But you have got to learn to let some people go *cheerfully*! So furthermore, the process is designed to expose the authentic *and the imposters*!

There will always be a process to endure in order to arrive at the destiny God has for you. And as we go through this process we learn that our destiny is not a place or an end to your journey—that's not what this life is about. It's not about running through your life like a horse—trying to get to a certain place with still enough time left to enjoy it before you die. But *your destiny is the journey* you were a created to travel. And how you handle the journey determines the quality of your destiny. Repeat after me "My destiny is the journey".

As you find your place in the process, you'll find out just how mature you are in the area of *patience*. Newsflash: People *with vision* are most times tormented *by the vision*. They are tormented because they have to constantly look at *what is* while waiting for *what is to come*. It's easy to get frustrated about the mansion God has promised you when you are still sleeping under a bridge or in your car. It's easy to get frustrated about the promotion when you are still bagging groceries at Kroger.

> Write my answer plainly on tablets, so that a runner can carry the correct message to others. This vision is for a future time. It describes the end, and it will be fulfilled. It if seems slow in coming, wait patiently, for it will surely take place. It will not be delayed.
>
> **Habakuk 2:2 NJV**

It's easy to get disappointed while waiting for the vision to come. But the bible tells us that patience is a virtue. Galatians also tells us that it's one of the fruits of the spirit. But we must hold on to our perspective. Paul admonishes us in Romans 12:2 to *"be not conformed to this world but be transformed by the renewing of your minds—that we may prove what is that good and acceptable and perfect will of God"*. This means we cannot look at things the way the world sees it. In order to hold on to our perspective, we cannot become emotional.

Emotional is defined as "dominated by or prone to emotion". Say this aloud: "I will not be *dominated* or *manipulated* by my emotions". In order to hold on to our perspective we must pace ourselves as we walk out the process. It's easy to want to skip the assignment and go right to the graduation. But if you went straight to the graduation (if you went straight to the promise), you wouldn't have anything to shout about. You wouldn't appreciate the reward because it will have lost its value. And ultimately God would not get the glory.

So I am encouraging you today, don't get frustrated. Don't give up. Don't grow weary while "doing well". In due season, at God's appointed time, you shall reap a harvest of blessings... if you faint not. But I repeat again, you *must* find your place in the process. Most of us go through this life trying to accumulate or consume as much as we can. We try to accumulate as much money. We try to accumulate as much land. We try to consume as much from the earth as we can, because we feel like time is running out. Here is what God says, "The cars, clothes, shoes, homes—forget about it!! Pick up your cross and follow Me!!"

But here is something that will set you free from being such a consumer: The blessing is already prepared for you. Jesus said, "In my Father's house there are many mansions if it were not so I would not have told you." (John 14:2)

He did not say my father is *building a mansion*. What God has for you, is already *READY* for you!! God is not preparing a blessing for you. But instead God is preparing you for the blessing. There are some things that God is working *out of you*—to prepare you for where you are going. *I know* there is still some stuff you are working on. But the stuff you are beating yourself up about is not what GOD is trying to work out of you. It's not the lying, cheating, cursing, and drinking. Those are only symptoms of a deeper problem. The stuff God wants to talk you about is much more serious.

He wants to work out your broken heartedness, unforgiveness, and insecurity. He wants to talk you about that fear of abandonment you have been holding on to; the disbelief, the lack of faith, the selfishness, and the bitterness that you are sleeping with every night.

As a side note, some of you have not given your life to Christ because you are waiting to *get rid of the stuff*. You keep saying, "*I'm going to do it when I get myself together.*" But as long as you are trying to do it on your own, you will never get it together. God knew you could not do it on your own. That's why He sent His son. He sent his son to be an example for you and then die for you. He did all this to let you know that nobody can take your life from you, unless you lay it down.

Jesus taught us how to let it go and lay it down. He taught us how to release the broken heart and love those who were trying to assassinate us. He taught us how to forgive those who speak all matter of evil against us and instead of cursing them out, speak a blessing over their life. In His example,

Jesus taught us, to be sober-minded and not consumed by material wealth while on this journey called life, but to store up for ourselves treasures in heaven.

Don't you think Jesus could have had a mansion while he walked the earth? Don't you think Jesus could have spent his time in the synagogues making a name for himself? Jesus could have had 20 camels and rode in style with the disciples. Instead, Jesus recognized that there was much more at stake. It is important to note that Jesus had found His place in the process.

Jesus found out that he was only sent here to do what he saw the Father do. He found out that he was not sent here for foolishness and wasting time. He had a task to complete. He had a divine assignment. Jesus remained on the course he knew he was created to travel; no matter how painful or uncomfortable it may have been. He taught us, though it's easy to be distracted—when your heart is in tune with the Father, the Holy Spirit will keep you. The Holy Spirit will arrest you in your weakest moment, right when you are ready to quit.

Even as He lay down his life and hang there dying on the cross, Jesus was teaching us "only that which is done for God will truly last." And if you need proof consider this: His death, burial and resurrection have been a topic of discussion for well *over 2000 years*.

Jesus has released so much power to you. But you receiving it is not dependent upon how morally sound you can be, or how perfect you may perform. It's not dependent upon how many scriptures you can quote, or how many Sundays you make it to church. You receiving what God has for you is dependent upon you opening up your heart to Him and changing your mind. The longer it takes you to change your thinking and begin to realize that everything you could ever think or ask for is already done, the longer it will take you to receive it. The children of Israel wandered for 40 years because they refused to change their thinking. They kept themselves out of the promise.

I've made a decision to let go of yesterday. And so can you!! The stuff I did 10-15 years ago (bad habits, insecurities, fears) will not stop me from where I am going. My past will not dictate or determine where I am headed in life. Once I made the decision to not look back, God began teaching me how to not judge what I see today based on my previous experiences. It wasn't easy, but it was worth it. It's never easy when God is trying to change your entire perspective on life. We get so accustomed to abuse, abandonment, and being betrayed that when God is doing a new thing it's almost impossible to notice the difference. Things may look the same but they are totally different.

In 2012, a movie was remade called *"Total Recall"*. I loved the first make of the movie, but I enjoyed the remake as it provided a great new perspective. One of the characters, Doug Quaid (*aka. Mr. Hauser*), was searching to discover his true calling. Like many of us, Doug was seeking to discover his purpose for existence. He wanted to know, "how did I get here?" and "where am I going from here?" Let's look at this conversation between Matthias and Mr. Quaid.

*₄**Matthias**: Mr. Hauser, What is it you want?

Doug Quaid: I want to help you.

Matthias: That is not the only reason you are here.

Doug Quaid: I want to remember.

Matthias: Why?

Doug Quaid: So I can be myself, be who I was.

Matthias: It is each man's quest to find out who He truly is, but the answer to that lies in the present, not in the past. As it is for all of us.

Doug Quaid: But the past tells us who we have become.

Matthias: The past is a construct of the mind. It blinds us. It fools us into believing it. But the heart wants to live in the present. Look there. You'll find your answer.

Doug Quaid made the error far too many of us make. We look backwards to yesterday for answers. When our present circumstances don't live up to our hopes and expectations, we have a tendency to look backwards—trying to figure out how, when and where we went wrong. We desperately want to go back to the place where we made the wrong choice and try to go in the other direction. We all want a do-over. However, yesterday doesn't exist anymore. It is tragic to be so blinded by your past that you are paralyzed with fear. Even though you see the new life on the other side, memories of yesterday hinder you from crossing over to experience it.

Most times when we are going through a mind shift, we go through it kicking and screaming. But at some point we have to make up in our minds that no matter how hard we have to fight, we have to get a new mind.

Once you find your place in the process you must begin to *walk in assurance*. I believe God has already shown you what He wants to do in your lifetime. It is my prayer that you get to see all that He has in store for you. But you have to make a decision today to exchange your negative thinking with statements like:

- ❖ I'm not going to get in God's way anymore.
- ❖ I do not doubt God anymore.
- ❖ I'm not going to be afraid of the *"what ifs"* anymore.
- ❖ I'm not trying to meet anybody's expectations anymore.
- ❖ If it doesn't line up with what God has shown me about my life, then I'm not doing it.
- ❖ And I refuse to let people try to make me feel guilty about following God.

Anything you set out to do that God didn't assign for you to do, God does not have to promise your success in it. Time is priceless—once it's gone, it's gone. We don't have time, energy, or tears to waste on an issue or completing an assignment that does not belong to us.

We each have an assignment to leave a legacy to future generations. And I'm not just referring to financial wealth. Our unborn grandchildren are depending on us to leave them with a firm foundation of faith, discipline, and spiritual maturity.

Do you know that you are responsible for the spiritual success of the next 3 generations of your bloodline? What you do today, in your lifetime will be repeated for the next 3 generations. Your children's, children's, children should know what values your family stands for based on what you teach and establish today.

If your family is divided today, you are teaching your children that family doesn't stick together and family is not important. As a result, they will then repeat it with their children, and those children will repeat it with theirs. And eventually, somebody further down in your bloodline will come along and say, "As for me and my house we will stick together and protect the unity of our family". Then a new cycle will begin, but it will be going in a different direction. It only takes 1 person in the bloodline to make a decision to change the entire course for generations to come.

> Now all Glory to God, who is able, through his mighty power at work within us, to accomplish infinitely more than we might ask or think.
>
> ### Ephesians 3:20 NLT

Whatever you have dreamed about and prayed for, it pleases God to give you the desires of your heart. But I am challenging you now to begin to think outside the box. God is not trying to fit into your cookie cutter style blessing. God wants to blow your mind. But your mind must be ready. He will not release anything to you that you are not ready to handle. If you are still trying to fit in the crowd, He will not introduce you to the people who are supposed to be in your life. If you are still insecure, overspending and trying to impress people, he will not release financial wealth. If your heart is still broken by the last person you loved, he will not introduce you to the spouse of your dreams.

You have got to find your place in the process. Find out where you are supposed to be and what you are supposed to be doing. Get a revelation about what God wants to do in your life. This type of self-discovery may mean withdrawing from the crowd and the noise for a season to simply hear from Him.

Stay on course. Give God your all and don't hold back! Be courageous and walk in the assurance that He who has begun a good work in you will complete that good work!! Trust God's timing and *expect* a breakthrough. Dream BIG! But just remember God always dreams bigger!!

13

Your Time is NOW

Yesterday, you said, "I'll do it *tomorrow*". Today, you are dwelling on what occurred yesterday; the good, the bad, and the ugly *yesterday*. And then before you lie down tonight, the thing that you so desperately need to complete will whisper to you, and again you will mutter the pitiful word, "*tomorrow*". The relationship you said you need to reconcile, the book you need to write, the classes you need to take, the forgiveness you need to extend, the money you need to save, the money you need to give, all of these things are waiting for a *tomorrow* that never seems to manifest.

In an attempt to transform your thinking and also to get you into the place that you can begin to understand this one thing: ALL the promises of God are answered every moment you take a breath. Every morning when you open your eyes and see the light of day, His glory is being revealed *in you*. Prayers that you have prayed have already been answered. Riches have already been released to you. Doors have already been opened unto you. He has already given you the desires of your heart.

Now, some of you may grasp this immediately. And then some of you will have seeds planted in your mind to begin a revolution in your thinking. But my prayer is that as God enlightened the eyes of my understanding, He will do the same for you. God is about to reveal some things to you that are downright devastating.

In order to complete this book, I had to experience an excruciating pain like I have never known pain to exist before. Like Job, the enemy was roaming to and fro looking for a soul to devour. And like Peter, Satan had desired to "sift me as wheat". But since Jesus had already prayed for me, I am alive today to strengthen you. Because His grace is sufficient for me in my weakness, I have survived. It's only because God got the victory out of the worst tragedies of my life that am I allowed to be here on other side. So I will simply share a word to *enlighten* you and *encourage* you.

There are 3 very important points that will move you from existing in *today* to finally walking through the door labeled *tomorrow*. In order to complete this chapter, God had to pull me back into a secret place in Him. I have experienced God's drawing many times in my life, and it's not a pretty or very attractive thing to experience. When God draws us close to Him, the drawing is most times preceded by a lot of hurt, pain, shame, rejection, abandonment, persecution and etc. So when people carry on like they are just happily being drawn into His presence and for them it appears to be the most desired experience to have, I often wonder if the testimony is authentic. Even Jesus experienced a level of agony each time he slipped away to be with the Father. When God draws you closer to Him, silences you, and covers you under the shadows of his wings, He does it for this reason: for an exchange to take place. It is during this isolation that He will work to subtract and then add something to your life. He will many times add virtue to your faith. He may add knowledge to your virtue. Then, after He adds the needed qualities into your life, He will begin to multiply your blessings. It's like this: God prunes you, so that you may then bear fruit, which as a result will produce seeds of greatness, which you will plant in others! Each time you choose not to fight it and surrender yourself to this process, you are granting God the permission and access to continue His work in you. He will reveal wisdom that will change your entire perspective on the experience called *LIFE*.

> For it is God who works in you, both to will and to do for His good pleasure.
>
> **Philippians 2:13 ESV**

So let's go back to Genesis 1:1-2. The bible tells us, "In the beginning God created the heavens and the earth. The earth was without form and void, and darkness was on the face of the deep." (nkjv) Take note that the earth was created formless, void, empty, and dark. It was made this way. Man did not exist – therefore neither did time. Even after morning and evening were created and the animals had been created, there was no time. There was only NOW. If a Lion had asked a bear, "What time is it?" After turning his head sideways and giving a look of utter confusion, his reply would be, "What is time?" There was no past. There was no future to behold. There was just *NOW*!

In the last chapter, I shared with you a quote from the movie Total Recall: "Time is a construct of the mind. It blinds us and fools us into believing it. But the heart wants to live in the present. Look there and you will find your answers." Your heart wants to live in the *now*!

What keeps us out of *now*? Obscured images from our past and an obsession with the future. The past is a previous event or experience that has created a stained image in your mind. Luke 9:62 (nkjv) Jesus tells us: "No one who puts his hand to the plow and looks back is fit for service in the kingdom of God."

The disadvantage is that our minds will continue to replay those images like DVD's or reruns over and over again until you have totally lost sight of today. The stuff that happened in your past is over, it is finished. It cannot harm you anymore. That hurt happened at that moment in time.

Like many of you, I have struggled to get my mind to move forward. God said to me, "Kimberly, the problem is you are rehearsing the hurt from yesterday. Like a DVD can replay a movie, you are replaying the words that were spoken, the doors that were slammed, the betrayal that occurred, the tears that you shed—over and over in your mind. You live as if it is still happening today." God says, "You are rehearsing things that you cannot change!"

We do not have access to the past. Each time you attempt to go there you will hit a wall. The past is, like we have already stated, a collection of images in our mind. Yesterday cannot be fixed, you cannot even touch it. But *today* you have this moment; you have now.

God has something new for you in *now*. He is presenting new glory and new opportunities to you every day.

But you have got to get out of yesterday to enjoy it. Step into NOW!

The future is an anticipated event that has not yet occurred. It is still a projected image of the mind. In the book of Matthew 6:34, Jesus tells us, "take no thought for tomorrow, for tomorrow will take care of itself". But contrarily, many times, we are so busy trying to protect ourselves from future hurt and demise that we cannot even recognize or enjoy the love of *now*.

On the other hand, we are so unhappy with *now* and dissatisfied with our current circumstances that we begin to build up a strong resistance to *now*. We try to project ourselves into a place in our minds where we will have joy in the future, because we think it is not available to us now. But when we do this, we miss the daily bread of this day!

King David declared, "This is the day that the Lord has made, I will rejoice and be glad in it." God has not made tomorrow yet. So we cannot physically rejoice in it. As much as each of us would like, there is no time machine that will project you into another moment in time. Hear me in the spirit. We will never reach or touch tomorrow. When you go to sleep tonight and wake up again it will still be now. So because we are not in tomorrow yet, and we are not promised tomorrow—all we have is now. Rejoice in now!!

I am convinced that we all desperately desire to rejoice. Yet, the challenge for us today, what hinders our ability to simply rejoice—is the pain associated with letting go of what happened in the past. And in addition to that, we must also let go of the grip we have on a future experience. It's okay to have hope and a reason to push forward. Yes! We should set our mark and our focus on the prize ahead. But we must balance that hope with a humble rejoice for today. As you begin to focus on now, God will begin to open the eyes of your understanding.

As you struggle to get a grasp on the images in your mind, it is normal to find yourself at war with your mind. Your mind wants to remain in control. It's no longer me against the world. It becomes "me against my mind". When you start separating yourself from your mind, and recognize it is its own entity, you will discover that you and your mind are not the same. AHA! This was the single most irreversible discovery in my life. "I" and my mind don't think alike. My heart (or my spiritual being) was hungry and doing its best to embrace the blessings of today. I deeply desired to be free in the current moment. I'd see others happily living their lives. And I wanted to join in so bad; to just run, jump, play, laugh, and enjoy life in the present moment. But instead, most times in my life—I felt like the little abandoned and abused girl standing over in the corner, feeling unqualified and not worthy of the same joy. I didn't feel I was worthy of being at the party! I was imprisoned by my own shame and rejection. Sadly, I had experienced rejection so much by others that I began to reject myself! So much of my life has been under-lived due to the tricks my mind would play on me. My mind would replay these scenes from both past painful experiences and then torment me with overwhelming anticipation for what I want to see in my future. But let me tell you: A great future is created by a great now.

What you do in this now will determine the quality of the next now. Focus on the now of Today! Now is the time for you to be healed. Now is the time for you to be happy. Now is the time for you to *live, laugh*, and *love*. Not tomorrow, not yesterday, but *now*! Now I am not by any means suggesting that we cannot hope and have dreams or goals to work towards. We talk so much about what we are going to do in the future: But *now* is the time—tomorrow is not promised. Today is the day!

Hebrews 11:1 starts out with "Now Faith is". Move the word now to the end and you get "Faith is *now*"! Faith is the substance. You have the evidence if you've got faith. If you have faith then you have *now*. And vice versa, if you have *now* then you have *faith*. If you have one you have the other; faith and now are inseparable.

The bible tells us to speak those things that *are not* as if though *they already exist*. God wants us to call those things that don't exist into existence for today. Move, operate, and make decisions as if you are already there. Today—assume the position—*now*! As our minds create images of our future and replays images from our past, it is important that we do not synchronize with the effects of our minds. Do not become aligned with the images in your mind. They are not real! Whatever happened, whatever he did, whatever she said: let it go!! We must become synchronized with what God is doing in our lives today.

Most times we create positive images of a bright future, to motivate ourselves to perform better in the *now*. That's fine. But the images of a bright future should not be used as a mental escape from today. Whatever is going on in your life today you must face it—embrace it—make peace with it.

You must live it. Until you do, you will never appreciate the power of right now. Every moment God gives us is packed with His presence. So don't miss another current moment by focusing on the next moment. When you get to the point that you are so consumed by tomorrow that you cannot rejoice in what God is doing *today*, you have been cheated. We have no power until we get into now. You have no power in the past. You have no power in the future; you only have power in now.

> Then God said, "Let us make man in our image, after our likeness. And let them have dominion over the fish of the sea and over the birds of the heavens and over the livestock and over all the earth and over every creeping thing that creeps on the earth."
>
> **Philippians 2:13 ESV**

Can I go a little bit deeper? We are spiritual beings having an earthly experience, right? Before He formed us in our mother's wombs, before we had a brain or a mind, He knew us, *right?* So this body that our spirits are housed in, along with this brain in our heads, is part of the things of the earth.

If God gave us dominion over everything in the earth and on the earth, then don't we have dominion over our own minds? It is important that we begin to take authority over our minds. We don't have to pray to God to take charge over our thoughts. He already gave us dominion—which is power to *rule* and *control*.

2 Corinthians 10:4 tells us, "For the weapons of our warfare are not carnal, but mighty through God to the pulling down of strongholds, casting down arguments, and every high thing that exalts itself against the knowledge of God, and bringing into captivity every thought to the obedience of Christ." What is a stronghold? A stronghold is an oppression and dominion of the mind. Consider this: Your mind has been oppressing you. Your spirit has been oppressed by your mind. I'm speaking to your spirit right now: WAKE UP!! God wants you to take back your power. God has not given dominion to your mind. He gave it to you! God gave us dominion *before* He formed us. But we must understand that He gave it to our spirit. He gave the power and authority to our spirit—not to our flesh or our carnal minds. Your spirit (the God in you) is in control!

Once I understood this, I began to view all other scripture totally different. I wanted to just read the bible all over again. That's why, "Greater is He who is in us, than he who is in the world". It's not we who are great, but He who is in us. That's why "we have this treasure in earthen vessels." The treasure is not the vessel itself, it's *in* the vessel (your mind is a part of the vessel itself.) Your spiritual being, in Christ, is the treasure in the vessel. So let's review this again. If God gave us dominion over everything upon the earth, that includes the vessel...right? You have dominion over your mind. So you have the power to take charge of your thoughts and the authority to bring them into captivity!!

In Romans 7:15 Paul tells us, *"I do not understand what I do. For what I want to do I do not do, but what I hate I do."* But then over in 2 Corinthians 12:7 Paul tells us, *"To keep me from becoming conceited because of these surpassingly great revelations, there was given me a thorn in my flesh, a messenger of Satan, to torment me."* Paul got an understanding and clarity. That thorn kept him in the now. That thorn reminded him of today. He had learned to be abased and abound, hungry and full. He had become content with the now. He wasn't focused on the past, back when he was royalty. Nor was he obsessed with when he would get there again in the future. He had that thorn in the flesh, a present day pain, to keep him in now!!

Then Paul went on to tell us, *"It's not that I have already apprehended the prize, nor have I been made perfect. But one thing I am doing (right now) I'm letting go of yesterday and pressing forwards towards the mark."* (Phil. 3:14 emphasis mine) He was not stressing about tomorrow. But he was pressing forward today (in the *now*) for a greater tomorrow.

Whatever state you find yourself in today is a reflection of what was going on in your mind yesterday. When Paul tells us, "Let this mind be in us, which was also in Christ Jesus" (Phil 2:5), he was referring to a mind under control and submitted to his own authority. Jesus kept His mind under control. He got away from the crowd, the disciples, and the people walking closely with him to renew his mind. That is to bring it under submission daily. If you can be like Jesus and control your mind—you can change your life!! There is actually no other way!!

Then God said, "Let us make man in our image, after our likeness. And let them have dominion over the fish of the sea and over the birds of the heavens and over the livestock and over all the earth and over every creeping thing that creeps on the earth.

"Philippians 2:13 ESV

Getting through the open door requires an enormous amount of courage. What keeps us from going through the door is the minds tendency to meditate on former things. But God says in Isaiah 43:18 "Do not remember the former things." And I've got to admit; even I have discovered that's hard to do. It sounds good and easy; we've turned it into a catchy cliché. But when you really begin to attempt to turn that mind power off, you face so much opposition—*internal and external.* So for those of you who have gotten through the door, I commend you! Only you know the tears, the disappointments with people, and heartache you've experienced to press your way through. But once you get through the door, the chains are broken!

To those of you who are struggling to make it through the door, looking back at your past with tears, God wants you to hear Him clearly, "What should have killed you, I wouldn't let it! When you should have drowned, I held in you the flood. I am doing a new thing and I am declaring it right now. But in order for us to go through that great door together, you must first get to *the now* with Me."

14

Don't Stop Here—Keep Going—Finish the Race

There are people who paid an expensive price for you and I to be where where we are today. Somebody died. Somebody was beaten. And some groups of people gave up their human rights and were treated like animals so that we could one day have the *hope* of living a better life. And because of their expensive sacrifice, we have their resilience as evidence of our own strength.

Since we have our predecessors as witnesses, they are our evidence that God created mankind with the ability and the capacity to lay aside the things that work to keep us from finishing the course set before each of us. The lives of those who came before us, is our evidence that we have the strength it takes to conquer the things that seek to conquer us. Their lives tell us, "God created each of us with the strength to stand and the power to endure." Most of us did not have to endure what the Children of Israel, African slaves, and the Jews had to endure. So if they could endure the chains, the beatings, the killings, and having their families torn apart, surely we can stand against the persecution, divorce, and live a day without our i-Phones!

Surely we can give up our comfort zones and fight the good fight of faith. Surely we can wipe the sweat from our brow and continue the remaining laps of our race.

> Therefore we also since we are surrounded by a great cloud of witnesses, let us LAY ASIDE every weight and the sin that so easily ensnares us, and let us run with endurance the race that is set before us Looking unto Jesus who is the author and the finisher of our FAITH, who for the joy that was set before Him endured the cross, despising the shame, and has sat down at the right hand of the throne of God
>
> **Hebrews 12: 1-3 NKJ**

Notice in the scripture, it tells us to lay aside the *weight* and the *sin*. They are not one in the same. The weight is that heavy burden that captivates our thinking. The weight is the past. The weight is the insecurity. The weight is disappointment. The weight is the OPP, which means "Other People's Problems!" The sin, which speaks for itself, is anything that separates us from God, anything that tries to become God in our lives. It is anything that distracts us from the love of God. It is anything that causes us to hide ourselves from God. It is anything that causes us to go in any direction opposite of the path God has designed for us to go.

It's not just the sex, or the lies or the murdering, or the cheating. It's the desire to do anything different than what God instructs you to do. The things that take our focus off of Him are sin. Sin is simply missing the mark God expects you to hit!!

So the author tells us to simply lay it aside because it has "easily" ensnared us. Notice the author didn't say the stuff you are "struggling with"—or the sins and weights that you have fought to be free from. He said that they *easily* ensnared us. The author is suggesting that basically we walked into the trap on our own.

We weren't kicking and screaming on our way into the traps of sin. We went willingly. It's like being compared to going fishing, and the fisherman didn't have to bait the hook. He didn't even have to cast his rod. The fish just jumped out the lake and landed in the net. How many of you know what I'm talking about? You know the times when you trouble didn't have to find you? You went looking for it—and found it right???

Over in Romans, Paul quoted, *"that which I don't want to do, I do—and that which I want to do, I do not do."* That didn't sound like much of a fight to me? At this point in time sin was having its way with Paul. And he wanted to figure out how to be free from the slavery of sin. Then a couple of chapters later in Romans Paul said, *"I beseech you* (to *beseech* is to beg) *therefore, brethren, by the mercies of God, that ye present your bodies a living sacrifice, holy, acceptable unto God, which is your reasonable service."* Romans 12:1 KJV.

I believe Paul must have heard Jesus whisper in his hear, "It's not about you, take up your cross and follow me." Because that's exactly what Paul did. He laid aside the weight of self-centeredness. He embraced the burden of ministry. He began to deny himself the right to complain or quit daily. He put *this* down, and picked *that* up. He put *sin* down—and he picked up *Christ*. Whenever he wanted to put the cross back down—when he wanted to put Christ back down, He told His body "NO".

> Pray also for me, that whenever I speak, words may be given me so that I will fearlessly make known the mystery of the gospel, for which I am an ambassador in chains. Pray that I may declare it fearlessly, as I should
>
> **Ephesians 6:19-20 NIV**

We must become like Paul and trade the chains of sin for the chains of God. To ensnare, is for someone to set a trap and lure you into it with the goal of possessing you and to have total control over you. Rats are ensnared. My uncle is a very skilled hunter and fisherman. My oldest son was blessed when Uncle Herman took Tramayne under his wings and shared with him the skills needed to become a skilled hunter. They hunt deer, squirrels, and many other rodents I care not to mention. These animals are all ensnared.

They are not chased and captured with a rope. But a trap is set for them with something that the animal is vulnerable to; normally some type of food. And as they are minding their own business, going about their own way they come across the thing that is normally a weakness for them. And as they begin to indulge in the bait that was set in the trap, the hunter has easily captured or ensnared the prey.

The enemy has a plan and clever a trap set for you. His plan is to put something along your path that would normally be a weakness for you. And as you are minding your own business, enjoying your life—that thing that "you think" you need will be sitting there waiting for you to indulge in it. And as soon as you do the enemy will have easily ensnared you.

God says, "I know the plans I have for you!! I have great plans to prosper you; to give you a hope and a future. I have an expected end in mind for your life. But you have to keep running in order to see what the end is going to be!! It doesn't matter which place you finish in, but you must finish."

So let us run with endurance the race that is set before us. Whatever race God has set before you to run, He has already given you the strength and the power to run! No matter who tries to trip you up, no matter how tired you get, no matter who is looking or laughing at you—*keep running*. No matter how many times you stumble and bruise your knee—*keep running*! No matter how far everyone else is ahead of you—*keep running*! No matter how much smarter they are, or how much more money they have than you—*keep running*! Keep your eyes on God—He is the author and the finisher of your faith. When you get tired, He kicks in and finishes the last leg of the race. So keep your focus on the cross. Don't get distracted from the prize. Don't stop! Don't quit! Don't throw in the towel—don't give up the race—*keep running*!! The race is not given to the swift or to the strong, to the educated, or to the rich. But this particular race is set before all of those who recognize they already have the strength, the courage, and the will to endure until the end. This particular race is set before those who recognize they don't need superficial gifts and talents, but a solid internal assurance. God has begun a good work in you, and you shall complete it! Nothing will stop God from getting you to His expected end. Keep running and finish the race!!

> I have seen something else under the sun:
> The race is not to the swift or the battle to the strong,
> nor does food come to the wise or wealth to the brilliant or favor to the learned; but time and chance happen to them all. Moreover, no one knows when their hour will come: As fish are caught in a cruel net, or birds are taken in a snare, so people are trapped by evil times that fall unexpectedly upon them.
> Ecclesiastes 9: 11-12 The MSG Bible

15

You've Already Won the Battle

Only you and God can truly know what you had to come through to get where you are today. Nobody but you knows the temperature of the fire you were in. But there is still yet another door God wants you to pass through. As you get ready to pass through the door, I want to warn you. As you are looking for the adversaries, beware the fact that many times the adversary just might be *you*.

Jesus told the disciples, "I have come that you would have life, and have it more abundantly!" But the tragedy is many of us never get to experience that abundant life because of our own hang-ups. Most of us are held back by our own inhibitions. Have you ever been afraid that you *just might* be all that you dreamed of? When we stay caught up in yesterday's success and failures, we hinder our own progression.

God is taking us somewhere; He wants us to experience all the goodness in life He has prepared for us. But we will **never** experience the fullness of God's love for us until we learn to process all of the hurt, all the pain, the betrayal, and the disappointments. God has shown me that when He does something it's never in our time or in our expected season. But He does things at His set and appointed time.

If we are still holding on to past hurts and disappointments when He performs a miracle, we will be forced to catch up to God. Have you ever had God to do something for you, before you were ready? Here you were minding your own business. You had probably given up on praying for the thing. And had just become complacent with where you were in life. But then when you least expected it, God shows up and drops a blessing in your hands so big that you can barely hold it. You may struggle to believe that it was God. You struggle to believe your eyes. But I am here to tell you: that day is coming! God's got a blessing for you so big that you won't have room enough to receive it! If it's a job you are seeking, a home, a family; God's got it in store for you! If it's your disability benefits or something as intangible as good health—God's got it waiting for you!

> For a great door and effectual is opened unto me, and there are many adversaries
>
> 1 Corinthians 16:9 KJV

But we won't get there until we face the giants in our own minds. The #1 adversary that keeps us from going through the door is unforgiveness. The disciple Peter tells us, "Be sober, be vigilant; because your adversary the devil, as a roaring lion, walks about, seeking whom he may devour." *(1 Peter 5:8)*

Satan knows that if he can devour you with his schemes, he can keep you from walking through the door. He knows that if he can trip you and make you fall on your way to the door, then the promises of God won't be fulfilled. Therefore, He constantly roams to and fro, looking for the right soul. Satan always looks for the souls of people who are not walking in the spirit. If you are not walking and living in God's spirit you can be attacked, approached and distracted by any of Satan's schemes. When you are not operating with a keen sense of discernment, it is easy to be deceived by his illusions. It's important to note here that since we are easily misled, he doesn't have to get clever with new tricks and schemes. He just uses the same ones over and over again. And the tricks will work every time on those who are not aware of them.

So I am going to give you four of the enemies most commonly used and successful schemes so that you will be aware of them:

- ❖ **Isolation**: The enemy uses isolation to keep you from walking boldly through the door. Deuteronomy 25:18 reads, "Those who strayed behind the group got attacked". When you are stranded outside the tent and isolated from other believers, the enemy can easily attack your mind and begin to play games with you. That's why the bible tells us, *"forsake not the fellowship of the brethren"*. There have been seasons in my life that if I were not coming to church and being around other believers, I would not have made it out of my darkest seasons and back into the light. There will be some times in your life when you just might have to make it on somebody else's faith. Sometimes you can be so hurt and broken that you just might have to survive off of the prayers of others. You can be so hurt or disappointed that you don't have the strength to believe. But the fact that others believe *for you* is what will bring you back to having hope again. King Solomon advised us that: *Two are better than one; because they have a good reward for their labor. If either of them falls down, one can help the other up. But pity anyone who falls and has no one to help them up.* (Ecclesiastes 4:9-10 NIV)

- ❖ **Intimidation:** Satan wants you to think your problem is too big for God. He wants you to think God is not interested in your issues. He wants you to think that God is surprised and was not prepared for your tragedy. But the truth is that God already knew and He already has a plan. Many times we end up spinning our wheels trying to resolve our problems in our own might and strength. This is why we never enter the purpose God has for us. When we try to become God and fix the problem instead of giving it to Him—that keeps us out of the promise. It also keeps God out of the problem. He can't release His blessing over what you don't release to Him. The word of God tells us that the battle will not be won by our might and strength, but by His Spirit. The Apostle Paul also tells us that, "Greater is He who is *IN US* than He who *is IN THE WORLD.*" So it's time that you look at your enemies and say, "There is greater in me!!"

- **Manipulation**: Manipulation is simply this: mind games. And Satan loves to play them! He is the master of all mind games! If he can maintain control of your mind then you will continue to be defeated by memories of your past, condemnation, and inadequacy. And he uses your mind as the tool to project these illusions. For some of you, the hardest thing to do is to seize the power of your mind. It is possible to want to do right and attempt to do the right thing. But as you keep rehearsing flashes of your past and how things use to be, you end up back there instead of going forward through the door. The enemy will actually manipulate you into thinking that the days behind you were greater than the days ahead of you. No matter how bad it felt. No matter how much you cried, the enemy will have you focused on the brief experiences that were good back there. And soon you will find yourself trying to recreate a moment that God wants to deliver you from. But the word of God reminds us several times in His word that our best days are ahead of us—not behind us. God doesn't repeat himself; He exceeds himself. Each time He moves us from one stage in life to the next, He does it differently and better than the last time. This is what is meant by the phrase "from *glory* to *glory*". He goes from great to greater to greatest—and then to "Greatest of All Time" (G.O.A.T.)! So as a result, when you place your life in His hands, your experiences can only show continuous improvement.

- **Condemnation**: Have you ever heard the phrase, "throwing stones then hiding your hands behind your back?" Well that's what the enemy does. What the enemy wants you to believe is that it was ALL your fault. He is skilled at creating snares to trip you on your journey. Then when you fall, you hear him laughing in the background. The enemy will shoot you, and then dare you to bleed. He will break your heart, then deny you the right to cry or grieve what was stolen. He wants you to feel ashamed for falling while being misled to believing it was your fault. Guess what? He knows he did it!! This was his plan from the beginning. If you allow him to trip you up then blame you for the fall, then he will have succeeded at his game. Satan is the great accuser of the brethren. And he spends his time night and day doing just that—accusing you! (Rev 12:10). People were drawn to Jesus because of his display of compassion. So if there is anyone in your life that seeks to tear you down by accusing *you* instead of the real culprit himself, if they lack compassion, show them the door! That is the spirit of the enemy.

Let it go! If Satan came to steal anything, it was your joy. He knows as long as you are focused on what you did back then, what you should have said, or could have done differently—you will never experience the grace of God. You will never become *whole*. The enemy wants you to enter into a perpetual state of depression. And once you let him in, then he will cause your depression to grow. One minute you are crying about the spouse, the next you will be crying about the kids, then it's the job and before it's all over you feel utterly worthless! In God's presence there is joy. There is absolutely no reason for you to feel ashamed or degraded because of your past. If you are in His presence, it is impossible to not be aware of His grace. God's grace is sufficient for you even in your darkest hour. His love pays for all of your shortcomings and setbacks. His love keeps you connected to Him even when you think you have royally screwed up! It is important for all of us to get to the other side of the door, to see just how much greater God is. God's power is greater than anything you could imagine. So let's G-O! Now is the time for you to seize your VICTORY!!

16

The Enemy, The Soul, & The Promise of Hope

No matter where you find yourself in life, no matter what stage or age, you will encounter the battle over hope. At times you will find yourself full of hope, and yet other times in deficit of hope. At times you will find yourself excited about having hope, and then other times afraid of the word hope itself. But no matter what end of the spectrum you find yourself, there will always be an inward pull of your soul dragging your burdened heart back in to the ring to battle over the your right to possess hope.

What is hope? If we asked Webster's we would find that hope is: *to cherish a desire with anticipation.* For example: hopes for a promotion, hopes for a new home, hopes for a job, and hopes for a new family. Strong's Concordance repeats the synonym of *hope* as *expectation.* And then it goes further to tell us that to hope is to dance or whirl, or to flee. How many of you know that when your back is up against a wall, and you feel your dreams have been destroyed, the one thing you must fight to seize is a shred of hope? The modern day psalmists *Mary Mary* sings a popular song so well:

The Enemy, The Soul, & The Promise of Hope

"I just can't give up now,

I've come to far from where I started from.

Nobody told me that the road would be easy,

and I don't believe he brought me this far to leave me."*5

We must put our hope in Him. The Bible tells us, "be anxious for nothing, but in every situation, by prayer and petition, with thanksgiving, present your requests to God…" (Phil. 4:6-7 nkjv) In the Old Testament, the prophet Ezekiel asked, "Can these dry bones live again?" Here, the prophet implies the need to regain hope for the resurrection of a dead city. Sara had reached a ripe old age of 100, when the promise of a child was about to be manifested. But she asked the angel, as she laughed in disbelief, "How can a woman my age have a baby? I'm old and worn out."

Neither of them had hope or a belief system that would allow them to fathom the possibility of *change*. But God used their disbelief to prove to you and me that, by faith and with hope, things can and will change!! So I want to talk to you about the 3 aspects of hope that we should become familiar with.

- ❖ The Enemy of Hope: Fear & Doubt
- ❖ The Soul of Hope: Expectation
- ❖ The Promise of Hope: God's Word—*LIFE*

Habakkuk's vision was carried by hope. God told him to write the vision so that when somebody reads it, they will indeed interpret the vision and run to perform it. God says "I've given you the vision, now don't procrastinate to put it into action. *Get moving!*" Even though things appear bad, and you are feeling defeated, you must have an assurance bubbling up from a reservoir of hope buried deep down inside of you to *keep* you running.

When I didn't know what hope was, God ignited a passion in me which drew me closer to the promise. Whenever I felt like I was utterly defeated and had lost everything, each time God reminded me that He intends for His promises to be fulfilled in my lifetime.

I was a motherless child who left home the first time at 13 years old. I never knew my father and my mother did not have the patience for raising children. So you can probably imagine that I experienced a very confused and rejected childhood. But I refused to allow abandonment to be my excuse for not going after *life*. I could clearly see that there was a life to be *had*. And my rough beginnings just meant that I would have to work a little harder than others to get there. As an innocent child, I never once believed that I wouldn't make it. When I didn't know what to expect out of my life, God gave me a glimpse of who I could become. So every time things became hopeless, He would take me back to the vision—reminding me of who I could become. Then, again I would be fueled with passion and HOPE to succeed.

The Enemy of Hope: Fear and Doubt

When God gives you a vision, He gives you an expectation of it being fulfilled. Then you continue to be drawn to it by hope. Yet, the number one enemy of hope is fear. You cannot have both at the same time. Fear and doubt are the direct opposite of hope.

What is fear? Fear is "false evidence appearing real". Fear is the ability of the mind to project an image of the worst possible outcome and then synchronizing your expectation and emotions with that negative outcome. In other words, fear is: believing the lie. We are not talking about the effects of fear like worry, stress, and outbursts of rage. But fear itself is rooted in believing a lie. If you want to overcome fear, find out the truth. You must find out what God says about the matter and synchronize your expectation and emotions with the truth.

And what is doubt? Doubt is simply to lack confidence. God says in Jeremiah, "For I know the plans I have for you, plans to prosper you and not to harm you, plans to give you hope and a future." (Jer. 29:11) When you don't know the truth about who you are and God's plan for your life, it is easy for the enemy to creep in and destroy your life with fear. If you don't know that in the end *you win*, the enemy will continue to suggest to you the lie that you might not make it. Then once you stop believing, you will stop praying.

Once you stop expecting to win, you will eventually stop running the race. When you have a hope for something the enemy's goal is to get you distracted; causing you to reach for things or people that look like the promise. Then when things don't work out according to the vision God has shown you, he will begin to manipulate you. Hope acts as a guard, a wall, and barrier for the promises of God to be fulfilled in our lives.

The Soul of Hope: Expectation

So the enemy is saying, "If I can just get him to stop hoping, I can get in his mind. If I can just get past this wall of hope, I can manipulate him to believe that he is already defeated—then I won't have to beat him at the race, he will simply give up the race and stop running!"

> Therefore do not cast away your confidence, which has great reward. 36 For you have need of endurance, so that after you have done the will of God, you may receive the promise
>
> **Hebrews 10:35-36 NKJV**

When Satan has made a breech in your wall of hope, you will begin to lose confidence in, or doubt, the vision. You will start thinking thoughts like, *"Maybe I expected too much"*, *"Maybe that wasn't the right vision"*, and *"Maybe I heard God wrong"*. But I have learned whatever God says to you directly, you better believe it and let no devil rob you of your hope for the promise. It *will* be fulfilled.

On more than one occasion, I thought my dreams were crushed. I had written the vision. I planted a seed on it in the offering plate. Then I called out my expectation. I was in full belief of the manifestation. But everything would fall apart and I cried out to God saying "Lord I don't know what to expect anymore—I don't even know what to pray anymore."

But that's where the enemy of hope wants you to be, in doubt and in fear of the unknown. He knows that in order for you to get to the promise, you must have hope. You cannot run this race without it. If he can get you to lose hope and not pray about the vision he can take you even further off course. And you will never reach the promise.

The Promise of Hope: LIFE

Hope is like an alternator. Once I was having a couple of problems with my car. For several months I would be driving it and while sitting still at a red light for some reason it would attempt to shut down. But as soon as I'd press the gas and give it the command to "GO" the car would keep going. Well the problem continued to get worse. And when I would turn the ignition key, it almost didn't want to start. So I took it to the mechanic to be tested. The first person tested my battery and said "Mam, here is your problem, you battery is registering extremely low". He gave me the cost for the battery. But something in me said, "Something has to be draining it". The mechanic suggested I buy a battery on the spot. I told the nice man, "Thanks for the advice but I would like to get a second opinion." So I had a really good friend to look at it and found out that the defective alternator was draining my battery. The root of the problem is the alternator..

Hope functions like the alternator in my car. The alternator is a generator that produces a current or a force to cause the engine to run and keep running. When you crank the car, power is pulled from the battery to start the alternator to running. But the battery is no longer needed at this point. Therefore, I can disconnect the battery in my car and it will still be running as long as the alternator is good. So like an alternator, HOPE is a generator that produces a current or force that keeps me going.

Hope creates the force needed to get me up out of my darkest valleys and depression. Hope creates the force that gets me moving after a loved one has died. Hope is the force that tells me to keep going when I am confronted with racism and bigotry on the job. Hope creates the current that keeps me going when all havoc is breaking loose in my life. Without hope, I will shut down. Without hope *everything* will come to an end.

Without an alternator, and having only a good battery, you can turn the car on, the lights will come on, the radio will work, music will play, it will shine bright and pretty, but you cannot crank it. It isn't going anywhere. There are some people who are going through his life with a good battery, but no alternator. The lights come on, they look good, the music is playing and they are dancing the night away. But they aren't going anywhere!! Life doesn't change, it never gets any better. And as a matter of fact, since the battery will eventually die, their life gets even worse. Without hope they are only standing still; stuck in a moment of time.

There is a greater life *in front* of you. But it starts with a change on the *inside* of you. It doesn't start with money, a gas card, a hotel room or a hot meal. The life you were called to live as kings and queens in royalty begins *in you*. Once a change happens on the inside—your countenance and your entire outlook on life will change. The shackles will fall off your feet. The veil will be ripped from your eyes. The chains will fall off your mind.

Some of you have been fooled into thinking that it's too late for you—like the race is over and you have no energy left to fight your way back into life. But just as Ezekiel looked at the valley of dry bones and asked the Lord, "Can these dry bones live?" You must also look yourself in the mirror and ask yourself, "Can I live again? Can I hope again? Can I expect the promise to be fulfilled again? Can I expect my marriage be resurrected?" And the Lord will answer you, "*Yes You Can*!"

17

A Message to Challenge You

I want to take a moment to applaud you for living beyond your obstacles. It is not often enough that we celebrate and applaud the efforts of people who climb mountain after mountain; sometimes never reaching the top. Many people relentlessly *die* on the climb. But for you that are still with us, I feel it is necessary to congratulate you for how far you have already come. You didn't give up. The fact that you are still here means that you are still pushing forward and that is commendable. You are a champion in God's eyes!

God has been (and still is) an awesome God!! As you look back and just reflect on the doors that have been opened to you, you should marvel in wonder at just how good God is. Oh! How much He must love us. Oh! How faithful He has been in our lives.

Can't you attest to the fact that God has been good? Hasn't He kept you? Hasn't He fed you? Hasn't He made a way for you? Hasn't He opened doors for you? Hasn't He kept you alive? If He has, then it's time to give God the standing ovation He deserves. Give Him the praise He deserves. You ought to just wake up to tell Him, "Thank You! Lord, if it had not been for You—I don't know where I'd be. But You saw fit to bless me one more time. And I thank You for bringing me this far by FAITH!!"

But after we take the time to thank Him for all He has done *for us*, And all that He has given *to us*, we thank Him for all that He has put *on us*(some of us got new jobs, new clothes, new places to lay our heads, new husbands). But we must take this time now to consider what God wants to put *in us*!!

We can get so excited about and addicted to what God is doing for us that we miss out on what He really wants to do in us. The bible tells us, "Without faith it is impossible to please God". (Heb.11:6) So now God wants to know, "*When are you going to trust Me enough to allow Me to put something in you?*" God is saying:

- ❖ "They ask for the food, I've given them that."
- ❖ "They ask for the cars, money, jobs, homes-I can give them all that."
- ❖ "They ask for a mate, I'll give them that too."
- ❖ "But **when, when, when**......will they ask for what I really want to give them?"

God wants to put something so powerful *in you* that you will never have to ask for anything else.

> Jesus said, "Everyone who drinks this water will get thirsty again and again. Anyone who drinks the water I give will never thirst—not ever. The water I give will be an artesian spring within, gushing fountains of endless life."
>
> ### John 4:13-14 The MSG Bible

In essence, the message Jesus was trying to convey to the woman at the well was, "You are running over here and over there looking for that one thing that will keep the empty places in your heart fulfilled. But if you would just ask me for the water and stop drawing from these empty wells, I can fill you with something that will quench your thirst before you can say the word."

When we continue to draw from empty wells, we will always come up short. We will always come back thirsting for more and never finding ourselves fulfilled. Our thirst is never quenched. We will never experience the abundance of life Jesus spoke of.

- ❖ Seeking fulfillment from a job is drawing from an empty well.
- ❖ Seeking acceptance, justification, and validation from our friends and family is drawing from an empty well.
- ❖ Seeking security in our homes, cars, money, and the government system is drawing from an empty well.
- ❖ Seeking our hearts fulfillment in a marriage is drawing from an empty well.

But instead, we must come to the Father, seeking Him with all of our heart, soul, and mind. Only He can fulfill the empty places in our hearts and sustain us. In the bible we are reminded that, "He who seeks the Lord shall find Him, and he that knocks, his knocks won't go unanswered."(Lk.11:9)

So I am going to challenge you today to seek the Lord like never before. Seek Him with your whole heart. Knock on heaven's door with your prayers and faithfulness—I promise you won't get the butler. But the Lord Almighty Himself will open His kingdom lifestyle to you. And then once the door has been opened to you, I challenge you to ask God to pour a new wine in you. Ahhhh! See now we are getting somewhere. It's all about the wine. I'm declaring it right now: this next phase of your life will be a season of *New Wine*.

In the Scripture, Jesus described the way wine and the wineskins were handled.

> "Neither do people pour new wine into old wineskins. If they do, the skins will burst; the wine will run out and the wineskins will be ruined. No, they pour new wine into new wineskins, and both are preserved."
> Matthew 9:17 NIV

Jesus was referring to the scribes and Pharisees of his time. They held very strong beliefs in the traditions of the elders. They were very settled upon the old principles of self-righteousness, self-fulfillment, self-images, and self-validation. And like the old bottles made of leather, the skins over time were decayed, waxed old, and unfit for use.

Now Jesus compared these Scribes and Pharisees to the old bottles, because being natural men, they had never been regenerated, reborn, and renewed in the spirit of their minds; in their old nature, they were mere self-righteous professors of religion. They had never tasted the new wine of Christ.

What is new wine? The *new wine* is a symbol of the *new love, new favor, and new joy of God*. *New wine* is a symbol of a *new heart*. I can speak all day on this. But when you get a taste of new wine, your heart desires something new; the old stuff just doesn't rock you anymore. The new wine is considered to be clean and refreshing, free from hypocrisy, or ulterior motives. The new wine is considered to be generous because of its cheering and reviving effects. And also, new wine is not ancient, or old. Since the wine is newly produced, it is known for its purity, good flavor, and pleasant taste; just like new converts who have come to the knowledge of Christ. How many of you can remember how good God tasted when you first came to Christ? Consider this: because God's love is new to us every morning, then this means new wine is being produced every day!! When you first get the revelation of God's love for you *in you*—you walk totally different, you talk totally different, and you laugh a whole lot more. Life is just that much more pleasant.

New wine is known for its generous effects in reviving drooping spirits, refreshing weary souls, and comforting distressed minds. When we say new wine, we are not referring to a new doctrine, or a new religion. The gospel does not change. But, it is called new wine because it is newly and more clearly revealed by Christ and the word of God.

New wine causes us to recognize the blessings of grace which spring from the love of God. New wine is manifested when we recognize what God did for us by sending Jesus to walk among us as mere man. He was tempted by the same distractions known to all mankind. He was also crushed by the same emotional pains.

> Inside I am like bottled-up wine, like new wineskins ready to burst.
>
> Job 32:19 NIV

This new wine was *manifested* by the Gospel when Jesus became a pardon for our sins. This new wine was *created* when He got up on the cross and shed his precious blood for us. Then this new wine *reconciled* us back to God by making atonement for our sins. This new wine justifies us, as well as sanctifies us.

But the bible tells us clearly that the new wine is not put into old bottle. *That is forbidden!!* New wine was forbidden to be poured into old wineskins because the particles in the new wine would cause the bottle to burst. As a result, the wine would be spilled or wasted. Jesus wanted us to know that, "My blood is too precious, too expensive, and too valuable to be wasted on somebody who will not accept what I did for them."

Remember, new wine is like a new heart. Why would He give you "new" joy if you will just go back to the depression? Why would He put a new joy in the life of someone who doesn't understand the price that was paid for it? Why would He give you a new life without making sure you understood what to do with it. A life of abundance in the hands of a fool will waste it on selfish and unrighteous living. But a life of abundance, placed in the hands of someone who knows without His grace they'd be dead, can be always seen given as a sacrifice. You will see these people laying down their lives as a sacrifice for others. That is ultimately the purpose of new wine. You get new wine when you discover, it's not about you!

> Therefore if any man be in Christ, he is a new creature: old things are passed away; behold, all things are become new
> **2 Corinthians 5:17 KJV**

Let's dig a little deeper. What is *an old wineskin*?

- ❖ old garments
- ❖ old images
- ❖ old relationships
- ❖ old ideas
- ❖ old habits
- ❖ old dreams

Old wineskins represent the things we have used all our lives to cover up who we really are. Old ideals we used to create a false sense of self. Old wineskins represent those who refuse to embrace the current moment, regardless of the pain that comes with it—and instead, prefers to hold on to all the stuff from the past that they are familiar with.

Old wineskins are those who agree with their old carnal hearts and principles. As a result, when God tries to give them a new heart and a new mind, they fight and reject them; causing wisdom and authentic love to seep out. This leads to even deeper condemnation and greater regret.

A million dollars in the hands of a selfish unbeliever will end up rotting in a bank account or blown away on material things. No one would ever experience the love of God through them. No one would ever witness the power of giving through them. But a million dollars in the hands of someone who knows they were once homeless, once needed a job, once needing clean clothes and that it was God who lifted them up, will end up lifting others out of the same desperation they once encountered. If God gave a million to someone who is already selfish, He would do them more harm than good. The millions would be wasted and would kill *them* in the process!!

But instead, Jesus said we should put *new wine* into *new bottles*, and *both* are preserved. By "new bottles" he meant sinners, whom Christ compelled to convert by his grace. The Spirit regenerates and renews those who are made new creatures in Christ.

Characteristics of new creatures:

- ❖ New hearts to love and forgive the unlovable
- ❖ New minds that are led by the Holy Spirit
- ❖ New perceptions of light, life, love, faith, and holiness
- ❖ New eyes to see with, they are focused on Christ
- ❖ New ears to hear God's voice, a stranger's voice they will not follow
- ❖ New feet to walk with, towards Christ and in the Spirit
- ❖ New hands to work and worship with

Now if you consider yourself a *new wineskin*, then the love of God is manifested and shining brightly in your heart. New wineskins have truly received and understand the value of the Gospel of Jesus Christ. They also enjoy the spiritual blessings of walking closely with Him.

When you put *new wine* in *new wineskins*, both the gospel of Christ and the grace of God along with the person who receives it are preserved and put to good use. When you put *new wine* in *new wineskins*, somebody new gets saved from their life of desperation and regret. Someone is healed from their brokenness, and delivered out of their pit of despair.

Many of us live in a state of constant depression and wake up each day searching for someone or something to relieve us from the pain of our circumstances. We can go out and buy bus cards, open more shelters, and outreach centers. We can buy new clothes and donate out of our homes. But if something does not change *in us*, then the circumstances will never change.

When you get something *in you*, your lives will begin to change. Your appearance will become different and day by day you will become stronger in your relationship with the Lord. When you get something *in you*, you will begin to discover who you really are and what you are made of!! Discovering "who" I am in Christ has been the single most important revelation in my life. No one could take that insight away from me.

But when you settle for getting something on you, you are settling for a temporary solution to what will be a lifelong problem. Paul told us to fix our hearts on the things that are eternal, the things we can't see. Because the things we can see are only temporary. The money, houses, clothes, jobs, those are all temporary solutions. These are things *on us* and not *in us*.

The more I search the scriptures the more I understand that God wants us to see *Him*. His desire is for us to grasp who we are *in Him*. Not in the eyes of our spouses, friends, or family members. Not in the eyes of our bosses or society at large. God wants you to know that you are not broke. You are not raped. You are not abandoned. You are not abused, misused, or rejected. But you are His beloved; a royal priesthood. You are a vessel of honor. You are more than a conqueror. Paul even asked us, "Don't you know that your body is the temple of the Holy Spirit which dwells *in you*?" God is working *in you* giving you the desire and the power to do what pleases Him.

God is not trying to get something on you. He's trying to get something in you!! He is working to get new wine in you. But you keep holding onto the old wineskins! God says you might have been broke last year, but if you let me pour new wine *in you*, you will never lack again. Your spouse may have abandoned you, but there is new love already prepared for you. Somebody out there might have been addicted to crack or marijuana or alcohol the last ten years. But says, "God give me a new wineskin and I will fill you with an addiction for Me."

There is a greater life ahead of you. But it starts with a change on the inside of you. Your real breakthrough does not begin with a gas card. It doesn't begin with the next hotel room. It doesn't begin with the next business deal. It doesn't begin with an engagement ring. The life you were called to live as kings and priests begins with the work God wants to perform on the *inside* of you.

God wants to put something so powerful *in you* that you will never have to thirst for anything else. You will never have to search for love again. You will never have to search for acceptance again. You will never have to ask for peace again. You will never have to ask for joy again. You will never have to ask for understanding again. God knows what you need, before you need it. But when you come to Him and ask for the *right* thing, you get *everything*!! God's got more for you!!

Now, some of you may have been deceived into thinking it's "too late". You may feel like the race is over and it's "too late" in the game. You may feel like you have no energy left to fight your way back. But God says, "YES! YOU CAN LIVE AGAIN!" Just go look yourself in the mirror and start talking to yourself. Ask yourself, "Is it possible that I can live again? Is it possible that my dreams can still come true?" Then turn around and answer yourself…YES I CAN!!!

18

FROM WINDOWS TO DOORS

To all of you who feel cast out, rejected, and abandoned I am here to announce to you that this is the year of God's open doors! I know you are probably saying "Well I have heard this before, but I'm still in the same place I was several years ago." But the problem is that you did not walk through the door.

In the Bible, God closes out the Old Testament with a challenge:

> Bring all the tithes into the storehouse, That there may be food in My house,
> And try Me now in this," Says the LORD of hosts,
> "If I will not open for you the windows of heaven, And pour out for
> you such blessing
> That there will not be room enough to receive it.
> (Malachi 3:10 NKJV)

Then over in the New Testament, the Apostle Paul tells us that:

> "For a great and effective door has opened to me, and there are many adversaries."
> (1 Corinthians 16:9 NKJV)

God told us in the Old Testament that He would open windows for us. But it is important to notice that over in the New Testament, He reveals to the Apostle Paul that He had indeed done a new thing! He revealed to Paul that He had opened a *door*. You can get a much greater blessing through a door than you could a window, *right?*

God is not leading us to windows anymore! He doesn't want us merely looking at the blessings He has prepared for us anymore. He wants us to begin to walk through the door to obtain it! God says, "No more window shopping, it's time to cross the threshold and go through the door!"

See windows are not designed for us to walk through. They are designed for us to look through. Seeing something that should be yours but not having access to it can be torture. And it's also good for preparation. Sometimes we walk past beautiful boutiques of life and peer in at all the immaculate possibilities. But we only *look* through the window when we realize we are not prepared or simply cannot afford what we see. We stare through the window with hope and pass it by. But God is saying, "It's time to stop window shopping." It's time to stop *looking at* what God is going to do. It's time to stop daydreaming about what your future will be like. It's time for us to leave the windows and step over to the door.

God wants you to know that He has granted you with access. As you step over to the door you will recognize that you are now granted access to all that you saw through the window. Yes we all <u>know</u> and understand that doors represent access, and many of you have <u>received</u> access. But the mere fact that you are still staring through the window, tells us that you have not <u>believed</u> that you have access.

> But without faith it is impossible to please Him, for he who comes to God must believe that He is, and that He is a rewarder of those who diligently seek Him.
>
> **Hebrews 11:6 NKJV**

God says that, "This is the year I am expecting you to show me that you believe." You *say* that you believe, but never take any actions to exercise your belief. When you get hired on a job you don't tell the employer that I'll just wait for my first paycheck then I'll come and work for you. NO! They offer you a job, and make a promise to pay you on a certain date. Then you show up on Monday morning, ready to exercise your belief, that they will pay you—by working. So whatever it is that you have been looking for God to change in your life, whatever you have believed God for. This is the year that God is expecting you to show up at the door! Exercise your belief!

If you listen to media reports and everything going on in our time, one might think that God has left us. Many people die (or transition) around the end of the year. And some just barely make it into the New Year. Then right after the New Year's parties are ending there are still many who transition over into glory. The enemy would want us to think that God has forsaken us. But the truth of the matter is that God has not forsaken us; just like He said He wouldn't. Instead, He is breaking the tradition of showing us our blessings through windows and challenging us to get up off our behinds, walk over to the door, then cross over and walk through it!

Darkness comes as a spouse who abandons us, or when we lose a job. Darkness comes when a child goes astray or is incarcerated. Darkness comes when the doctor tells you you've only got a few months to live. And when you are in darkness, you cannot seem to find the door. But even if you are in darkness, I challenge you to thank God for the darkness! God does His best work in darkness! Why? God does His best work in darkness because that's when you are forced to exercise your faith. The doors that are open to you right now are faith doors! Only those who have the guts to trust God in the darkness will make it through to the other side.

It is your faith that captures God's attention! Quoting scriptures doesn't get His attention. But doing something that shows Him you believe His promises, even in dark situations, will cause God to turn His face towards you.

Here is another key note: These doors will swing right open even as you begin to approach them. You won't have to fight with the door. You won't have to work the door. All you have to do is make the decision to show up and every miracle and blessing that God has lined up will fall into place. People you would have never anticipated meeting will cross your path. Unfavorable situations will begin to turn around in your favor. But you have to believe for it!

> *Give, and it will be given to you. A good measure, pressed down, shaken together and running over, will be poured into your lap. For with the measure you use, it will be measured to you.*
>
> **Luke 6:38 NIV**

Some of us will be givers and some of us will be receivers. You cannot give what you don't have. So this means you must be in a position to receive. This year God is expecting you to get in position, get through the door and obtain what He has in store for you, so that you can give it to somebody else. This is not a selfish message. I repeat, *"This is not a selfish message"*. This is not the time to pray selfish prayers. This message is not crafted for you focus on *what's in it for you*. Choosing to remain in a position of lack and becoming complacent your current situation is a selfish choice.

Your walking through the door is not about you. But it is about the people God is expecting you to bless and lead out of their places of darkness.

And here is the important part: The door will not always be open. If you do not get up and walk through that door during your moment of opportunity you will miss out on God's plan. The opportunities that have been scheduled for you this year, you cannot get next year. You cannot call God and reschedule the appointment. Those blessings are scheduled for *this year*!

Let's take a look at how the man was healed at the pool of Bethesda:

> *Now there is in Jerusalem by the Sheep Gate a pool, which is called in Hebrew, Bethesda, having five porches. 3 In these lay a great multitude of sick people, blind, lame, paralyzed, waiting for the moving of the water. 4 For an angel went down at a certain time into the pool and stirred up the water; then whoever stepped in first, after the stirring of the water, was made well of whatever disease he had.[б] 5 Now a certain man was there who had an infirmity thirty-eight years. 6 When Jesus saw him lying there, and knew that he already had been in that condition a long time, He said to him, "Do you want to be made well?"*
>
> *7 The sick man answered Him, "Sir, I have no man to put me into the pool when the water is stirred up; but while I am coming, another steps down*

before me."⁸ Jesus said to him, "Rise, take up your bed and walk." ⁹ And immediately the man was made well, took up his bed, and walked. John 5:1-9 NKJV

Even the bible tells us that every event has a particularly scheduled time and appointed season for occurrence. The man lying at the pool of Bethesda knew that only once a year the waters would move. It would be only at that one specific time that he'd have the opportunity receive his healing. He knew that the opportunity was timed!

I am announcing to you, that you are currently in the season of multiple blessings at an accelerated speed. You are in the season of great increase and opportunity. God is challenging you to "Get up and get ready!" God has begun a *great* work in your life and He will complete His work. God is a finisher. He does not start something to walk away distracted and leave it undone.

But in order for His work to be complete, you must learn to obey his will. You must get up out of your dead situations. No matter what you have been taught, no matter what challenges you have faced up until this point—you are well able to possess the promise.

There is a better you *on the inside of you* ready to live. You have been afraid of that voice on the inside of you calling you to greatness. Some of you have been intimidated by your own purpose and dreams. You've sat at the window and seen the life you are supposed to be living. But fear and doubt have kept you paralyzed at the window.

Those days are over! This is not the season to keep staring through the window. You don't have another year to lie and wait for someone to put you in the pool. This is the year for you to take up your bed and walk! You will go through the door!

19

TAKE IT ALL BACK...
and Then SOME

It is time for you to *pursue* the promise, *overtake* your obstacles, and *recover* ALL that the enemy has destroyed! Not some, but ALL! It doesn't matter what you have lost, or what you will have to face on your way to recovery. But what you are going to recover is worth the pursuit. So get ready, because in this chapter you will begin to overtake every force that has held you back. And you will recover it all! The very thing that defeated you will become your place of victory!

Say these words out loud:

RESTORE—DOUBLE—INCREASE—FAVOR—WISDOM—LIFE—
HEALTH—STRENGTH—OVERFLOW

1 Samuel 30:8 reads:

> "And David inquired at the LORD, saying, Shall I pursue after this troop? Shall I overtake them? And he answered him, Pursue: for you shall surely <u>overtake</u> them, and without fail <u>recover all</u>."
> (Somebody say, "AND THEN SOME!")

Genesis 1:28 reads:

> God blessed them; and God said to them, "Be fruitful and multiply, and fill the earth, and subdue it; and rule over the fish of the sea and over the birds of the sky and over every living thing that moves on the earth."

All the way back in Genesis—God painted a picture of what life would look like for all of humanity. The first instruction that God gave to Adam and Eve was to reflect His image. Then the second thing He did was explain to them what that looked like. He said, "In order to look like Me, you must do these three things—1. Be fruit and multiply 2. Rule and Subdue and 3. Have dominion."

This is the time to PURSUE! So I pose this question to you, "What are you going to pursue *next*?" To pursue something means to passionately go after something important to you. When you pursue something, you are looking to take possession of it. You are looking to make it your own. You must be willing to push forward towards it with all of your might, power, and spirit. You must be willing to press past every locked door, climb every mountain, skip over broken glass on the ground, and with sweat dripping from your brow, *PUSH* towards the goal!! To pursue something means that you are willing to work for it. So what are you ready and willing to pursue?

Therefore, if you make up your mind to pursue something, this signifies the fact that the thing you pursue must be something of extreme value to you. Things that are pursued are not easily obtained. We have all heard the saying that anything worth having is worth working for—or fighting for. In order to pursue something you must have a strong *belief* that you are somehow able to succeed at achieving it. How can you *pursue* a goal if you do not believe you will reach it? No one in their right mind would go after something they did not believe they would achieve. The human mind does not work that way.

To pursue greatness—you must evict doubt. So God says, "If I can just get you to *believe* in a better life—then I can motivate you to *pursue* it". Many times when we pursue something, if it is something we want bad enough, we will be willing to lay aside all pride, order, and formalities to achieve it. How many times have you ever been so desperate for something that you didn't care if you had to cry, beg, or get ugly for it? In the book of Matthew, there was a woman who inquired of Jesus the Lord for a blessing. Yet, in the presence of others, Jesus responded to her that according to custom it would not be fitting for him to bless her. Yet she wanted and needed what he had so badly, that she positioned herself in the posture of begging to obtain it. She says, "That is correct, Lord. Yet, even the dogs eat the crumbs that fall from their master's table." *(Matthew 15:27 NKJV)*

To pursue something means that you lay aside any and everything that hinders your ability to obtain it. This means that you ignore the haters, the naysayers, and the non-believers. In order to fully pursue something you must be willing to travel the distance *alone if necessary*. To pursue something means that you are willing to make room for the thing you are trying to obtain. You clear your schedule. You make time to do the things that develop you and prepare you for your desired goal. You let go of toxic relationships. You let the people who are zeros or placeholders go! You clear your mind of the dirty laundry of yesterday. When you are ready to pursue a new life, you will get a revelation and then set your mind on all that God has shown you about who you are. You will keep your focus on that very thing. You won't lose the invention, the business idea, or the talent God has placed in you. You don't change your mind; you don't give up; you don't quit until you obtain it! To pursue greatness—you must *evict doubt*!

This is the time to OVERTAKE! Reverse the compound word and you get *take over*! This means it's time for us to subdue; which means to take control of something by *force*. To overtake something you must recognize that you are bigger, stronger, smarter, and better endowed than it! To overtake something, you must get the understanding that the thing that once had control over you, is now subject to you. I have a message for you straight from the Lord on high: You were created to dominate your world not have your world dominate you. To dominate means you win!! To dominate means that you are positioned to succeed wherever God has placed you. Whatever situation or circumstance you find yourself in, or job He places you on, you are to win. You are to be the leading force of power. You are to dominate!

I have been in the human resources and staffing industry for many years. And what I have witnessed, even in my own life, is that while hundreds of resumes are submitted for a job, only 20 or 30 (*most times much less than that*) actually get read by the recruiter. Then, approximately 5-10 will have their resumes placed in front of the hiring manager for review. Out of that, on 3-5 people are selected for a face-to-face interview. But at the end of the screening cycle, the only one that will get the job offer is the one who started with the confidence that says, "I got the job, I've already won, I have dominion!"

When I have accepted job offers over the years, I'd call my mother in excitement and share the great news. My mother used to be so baffled. She'd say, "Girl you *always* get the job, what are you saying or doing?" I never had an answer for her. But for me, when I got the email or the phone call to schedule the interview, my first thought is always: "Oh I got the job!" I trained my brain to never really entertain the idea that I might not get it. So if my resume makes it past hundreds of others and capture your attention, then you *actually read it*—Oh I am confident you are going to call! And when you call, I have the job!! That's just the way I think. That's the way winners think! That is a *dominion mentality*! The only decision I have to make is, "Do I want it?" So when I show up for the interview, I'm actually interviewing *them* to see if this is where God wants me to be! Don't worry I hear you. And then even if I don't get it, I just K.I.M (*keep it moving*) because God's got somewhere else for me to be.

In order to look like your heavenly Father, you must have dominion. There is nothing *in* this world or *of* this world that should be able to overtake you. You have the *power*! You have *favor*! You were created in His image. You have His spirit!

This is the time to RECOVER! What does it mean to *recover*? Recover means to take possession of what once belonged to you before. You may have lost it in repossession or divorce. You might have lost it in foreclosure. You might have lost it in sickness. But this is the time for you to take back all that God ordained for you to have from the beginning of time. Before God formed you, He blessed you! Before He formed you, He created a particular place and space in time for you. Before He formed you He fashioned all of your days for you. Before He formed you, your battles were already won!

So you think you lost it all in the fire of affliction? Once you fail, fall, and hit rock bottom, the worst has already happened! But what's most important is that you are *still here* to tell the story. People may have watched your downfall and pass you by on the street thinking you will never get up. But that's right where God wants you to be. Because when *He* lifts you back up, restores you and gives you double for your trouble, those same naysayers who wrote you off and left you for dead are coming back around. Just ask Job!

> Before I formed you in the womb I knew you, before you were born I set you apart; I appointed you as a prophet to the nations
>
> ### Jeremiah 1:5 NIV

This is the time to MULTIPLY! What does it mean to *multiply*? *[6] Webster's says that to multiply means "to increase in number by reproducing". Jesus gave us a great demonstration of what it means to multiply. John 12:24 reads, *"Truly, truly, I say to you, unless a grain of wheat falls into the earth and dies, it remains alone; but if it dies, it bears much fruit.*

In essence, the message Jesus was trying to convey is that everything starts with a seed. And when you know what to do with the seed (*you plant it*), then you will always get back more than you started with. Jesus was saying, some of you are going have to die or at least feel like you have died. You may feel like your dream has died. You may feel like your business died. You may have lost your spouse or the marriage died. You may feel like the job or the car died. Like Job, you may have lost it *all*!

Job 1:15-22 (NIV) reads:

"The oxen were plowing and the donkeys feeding beside them, 15 and the Sabeans attacked and took them. They also slew the servants with the edge of the sword, and I alone have escaped to tell you." 16 While he was still speaking, another also came and said, "The fire of God fell from heaven and burned up the sheep and the servants and consumed them, and I alone have escaped to tell you." 17.While he was still speaking, another also came and said, "The Chaldeans formed three bands and made a raid on the camels and took them and slew the servants with the edge of the sword, and I alone have escaped to tell you."18 While he was still speaking, another also came and said, "Your sons and your daughters were eating and drinking wine in their oldest brother's house, 19 and behold, a great wind came from across the wilderness and struck the four corners of the house, and it fell on the

> young people and they died, and I alone have escaped to tell you."... 20 Then Job arose and tore his robe and shaved his head, and he fell to the ground and worshiped. 21 He said, "Naked I came from my mother's womb, And naked I shall return there. The LORD gave and the LORD has taken away. Blessed be the name of the LORD."...

Do you notice that the first thing Job did after God allowed everything he had worked for to be destroyed was worship? He didn't take his life. This is for somebody reading this right now: Don't take your life. Stay in the game. God loves you and if you will trust God, and hang in there a little while longer I assure you that He will turn your mourning to dancing, and your sorrow into joy. He will turn your troubles around and you will make it through! Job didn't take his life. Instead, he remembered *who* allowed him to have it all in the first place.

Job 42:10 NIV reads:

> "The LORD restored Job's prosperity after he prayed for his friends. The LORD doubled everything that Job had once possessed."

And in the end, after he was tested in the fire of affliction, after he was tested in his marriage, after he was tested in his health, after he was tested in his relationships, after he was tested in his finances, he was restored a double measure of everything he thought he had before! God said, "What you thought you had before, that was only the beginning—I just needed to test you in the fire! You haven't seen my best act yet! Your set back was a set up! I am getting ready to restore you and multiply you!" In this story of Job's victory, we learn losers make the best winners! God says "If I can trust you to lose something and you are still here—then I know I can trust you to win!!"

As a child of God, you are expected to reflect His image. God's image has been tried and tested in the fire. When Jesus died on the cross, God's image was being tried in the fire. As Jesus emerged from the tomb—God's image came forth as gold. As a result, the kingdom was advanced and multiplied!

In order to exhibit the principle of multiplication, you must understand the principle of seed, time, and harvest. It is a requirement that you multiply or reproduce more of *Him* in the earth in order to fulfill your generational purpose. You're responsible for planting and sowing seeds that may take 2-3 generations to produce a harvest. Your children's children should be reaping the rewards of your life's work.

I'm going to challenge you here. Are you ready? Brace yourselves: If you are not multiplying anything or reproducing—God sees it as *REBELLION*. To sit on the sidelines of life and chill, while your days pass you by is sin. You were not created to chill. You were created to take dominion!

The time is now for you to begin to activate the principle of multiplication in your life. When you get up and move, a supernatural release of God's favor, wisdom, increase, and overflow will be accelerated in your life. We don't have any more time to waste on drama, doubt, or fear. We don't have time *to waste time*! God is moving and doing a new thing in this earth. But if you are going to be a part of the shift, you must be in tune and synchronized with *His plan*.

Get ready to pursue—Get ready to overtake—Get ready to recover—It *ALL*!!

20

A Shield of Favor

Many times it may seem as if you are in a bottomless hole. And the hole you are in seems to be getting deeper and deeper. Right here it is natural to grow weary in our attempt to pull ourselves up and out of the pit. But my assignment is to encourage you to fight! Your emergence from the despair and the deep dark valley you have found yourself in, lies in your ability to recognize that you have an unlimited amount of power, grace, and favor working for you. It is very important to keep this in perspective.

Make no mistake I am not merely referring to the weariness that comes along with being in a financial crisis. I am sure most of my readers can agree that it's much deeper than that. The emotional, physical, relational, and spiritual debt that we find ourselves in has the power to do much more damage to our belief system than money ever could.

Everybody has at least 2-3 enemies. And I am referring to more than just the people who you think are *"hatin'"* on you. We've all got our haters and naysayers. But our most powerful enemies are those that start from a much closer proximity to us. Our most powerful enemies lie deep within us. A poverty mindset, our addictions, our depression, our failures and shortcomings, jealousy, bitterness—are all things encompassed within us and hinder us from living the abundant life God intended for us to live.

King David reminds us that, when our enemies rise up and work against us, working to destroy us, it is the favor of God that will surround us like a shield. When the devil begins to throw fiery darts, piercing arrows and blind temptation at you, favor from God will block those schemes from reaching you. And most times the attack will boomerang and end up right back where it came from! How many of you know that the favor of God can cover and protect you, even when you can't protect yourself? The favor of God can protect you from enemies foreign and domestic; internal and external. The favor of God can protect us from attacks seen and unseen. There are plots against you that you know nothing about, even on the inside of you. But the favor of God is protecting you even when you don't know it.

In the story of David and Absalom *(2 Samuel 13-19)*, David found himself, his family, and his army on the run from his son Absalom. Absalom was a rebellious son whose one goal in life was to be made king, even if it meant disgracing and killing his own father. But what he didn't know was that even his rebellion, was a part of God's plan to bring David to a place of worship after his sins against Bathsheba and Uriah.

> And the Lord said, "Simon, Simon! Indeed, Satan has asked for you, that he may sift you as wheat. 32 But I have prayed for you; that your faith should not fail; and when you have returned to Me, strengthen your brethren."
> **Luke 22:31-32 NKJV**

Do you know if our enemies thought they were really helping us, they wouldn't waste their time trying to attack us? See this was an enemy David brought upon himself. How many of you have had to swallow your pride and admit at one point or another that "I brought this trial or setback upon myself?" You may have clearly heard God say, "Don't marry them!" But you went ahead planned the wedding and did it your way. You may have heard God say, "Don't do business with him, wait for Me to send you the right people." But in haste, you disobeyed God's warning. God will let you go as far as you think you can go, and you will finally have to admit, "I brought this on myself, now Lord I need your help!"

But even when we find ourselves in trouble that we created for ourselves, God is still faithful to cover us with His favor. Even David found out that a shield of favor will cover you better than ten thousand troops. A shield of favor will cause others in the enemy's camp to begin to work on your behalf.

Proverbs 22:1 NKJV reads:

> *A good name is rather to be chosen than great riches, and loving favor is better than silver and gold.*

Proverbs 12:2 NKJV reads:

> *A good man obtains favor from the Lord, but a man of wicked intentions He will condemn.*

Romans 8:38-39 NKJV reads:

> *For I am persuaded that neither death nor life, nor angels nor principalities nor powers, nor things present nor things to come, nor height nor depth, nor any other created thing, shall be able to separate us from the love of God which is in Christ Jesus our Lord.*

You can make your bed in hell, but the Lord will still be with you. Nothing can separate you from the love of God. Not your enemies, not your friends, not your family, not your sins. Nothing!! I don't care how bad you messed up. I don't care how far you think you have strayed away. I don't care how they laugh at you to see your marriage fail. There is not a single reason that would qualify you to be forsaken. God will never leave you alone.

Once you recognize and claim your inheritance as a child of the King, nothing can separate you from His love. What I have learned is that as long as I have His *love*, I have His *favor*!

When I look back over my life, I realize it hasn't been easy to walk in my own shoes. Most times, I have to encourage myself. I look in the mirror and I tell myself, "You are one *bad* momma!! Your life has not been a life for the faint at heart! But you continue to overcome!" I am convinced and I believe that it is His *favor* that has kept me when others have drowned in their sins and died from their attacks. It is His *favor* that has kept me working in the midst of recession. It is His *favor* that has kept my children clothed and fed.

It is His favor that opened doors for my children to attend college with scholarships and grants. It is His *favor* that has caused my enemies to fall into the pits they dug for me. Let somebody reach out to lay a hand on you and watch your Father reach down from Heaven and take them out! You and I both, we are covered in *favor*!! So let's flip over to Psalms to find out how David processed this attack from Absalom.

Psalm 3:1-4 NKJV reads:

> LORD, how they have increased that trouble me! Many are they that rise up against me! Many there be that say of my soul, "There is no help for him in God." Selah But Thou, O LORD, art a shield for me, my glory and the lifter up of mine head. I cried unto the LORD with my voice, and He heard me from His holy hill. Selah

David opens in anxiety and fear. Notice his posture. It's as if he is standing back looking at the crowd coming against him. Your crowd could be bills, legal issues, or a bad report from the doctor. But David is standing back in awe at the army of issues coming his way, thinking, "How in the world will I survive this one? If I make it through this one alive, God will have to do it."

Psalm 3:5 NKJV reads:

> I laid me down and slept; I awaked, for the LORD sustained me

Here after David has cried out to God all night, in fear and in worry, He finally decided to lay down. Tired and worn out from his tears, he slept as the Lord sustained Him.

Psalm 3:8 NKJV reads:

> Salvation belongeth unto the LORD. Thy blessing is upon Thy people. Selah

Then David remembers his inheritance from God. He closes Psalm 3 remembering the favor of God.

Psalm 4:1 NKJV reads:
> Hear me when I call, O God of my righteousness! Thou hast set me at large when I was in distress; have mercy upon me, and hear my prayer.

David once again opens in his posture of distress and anguish as he calls out to the Father for help! Check his posture now once again; he is in fear. Sounds like he took his eyes off the promise, right? Once again he's anxious and pleading with God asking, "Oh Lord how will I survive?" Now didn't he just close out Psalm 3 remembering His inheritance? Sounds like us right? We too have repeatedly gone back and forth. How soon we forget our inheritance when trouble arises! How soon we begin to feel small when the enemy stands tall against us.

Now hidden in the middle of this Psalm is a simple instruction from God that changes David's posture from standing in anxiety and awe to resting. God whispers to David in a small Selah voice:

Psalm 4:4 NKJV
> "Be angry and do not sin. Meditate within your heart on your bed and BE STILL. Offer the sacrifices of righteousness and put your trust in the Lord."

What are the sacrifices of righteousness? The Apostle Paul said *"present your body as a living sacrifice this is a reasonable service unto God" (Romans 12:1)*. There might be some things that I want to do that I just can't do. There will be some places that I will have to go that I just don't want to go. Who wants to be arrested? Who wants to be in jail? Who wants to be homeless? Who wants to be sick in a hospital bed—or even worse in hospice? We work to remain good citizens and stay healthy; to keep ourselves out of these positions. But many times being put in these circumstances is a reasonable sacrifice to God. He can use us anywhere He chooses!!

Psalm 4:7-8 NKJV reads:
> Thou hast put gladness in my heart, more than in the time that their corn and their wine increased. I will both lay down in peace, and sleep: for thou, LORD, only makes me dwell in safety.

David ends again in the safety of God's promises as he brings his tantrum to a rest. What promise? It is the Lord who promised, *"I will keep him in perfect peace whose mind is stayed on me."* (Isaiah 26:3)   If we can manage to keep our minds focused on the stability of God's promises, He will surely guide us through to safety.

Don't look to your left or to the right. Don't focus on what your enemies are saying or doing to get you off track. But lay down in peace, and *go to sleep!* Are you convinced that if you resist the devil that he really will flee? No matter how the enemy tries to take you out—no matter how many lies your accusers tell—no matter how big of an army your contenders build to fight against you, if you remember you are covered by God's shield of favor, the Lord will be swift to swoop down and rescue you!

Psalm 5:1-3 NKJV reads:

> Give ear to my words, O LORD; <u>consider my meditation</u>. Hearken unto the voice of my cry, my King and my God, <u>for unto Thee will I pray</u>. My voice shalt Thou hear in the morning, O LORD; in the morning will I direct my prayer unto Thee <u>and will look up</u>"

David now opens with a prayer, a song of meditation. He is a little more at ease. His worship is flowing much more freely. However, though he is still requesting an audience with God, he has found peace in his waiting. He still wants to be heard. But He is now resting in the promise. But if you will notice he closed Psalm 4 saying *"I will lie down in peace"* and does what? *SLEEP!* His spiritual posture has changed!! He is no longer consumed with fear and anxiety. He has stopped wrestling with the thing that brought him so much anguish. David is going back to sleep!

And after having slept through the night, at peace, in safety, meditating on his promises, morning comes. You didn't hear me. I said, *"Morning comes!"* In the morning David has awakened with the strength and the confidence to look up. David began Psalm 3 filled with anguish and awe at the obstacles ahead of him. But now over in Psalm 5 he has let go of the overwhelming fear and doubt. He is now worshiping the Lord.

Psalm 5:7 NKJV reads:
> But as for me, I will come into Thy house in the multitude of Thy mercy, and in Thy fear will I worship toward Thy holy temple.

In the middle of this Psalm, we now see David has finally moved to a place of total worship! Why do we have to press so hard to enter into a place of worship? We have all been attacked before. We have all been afflicted. But like David, we all experience a range of emotions (including pride, fear, and anxiety) before we enter into His place of rest and worship.

Psalm 5:11-12 NKJV reads:

> *But let all those rejoice who put their trust in You; Let them ever shout for joy because You DEFEND them; let also those who love Your name be joyful in You. For You O' Lord will bless the righteous; with favor You will surround him as with a shield.*

And here, David closes with the assurance he needs to stand in the midst of his circumstances *with the assurance* that he will be victorious. His confidence has been restored. He got up every day calling for the hand of God to move on his behalf. But he makes it through the storm and closes out with the evidence of God's favor. David recognized that, "It is because of God's favor that I am alive."

Many of you have seen sickness, experienced cancer, endured painful divorces, have seen jail time, lost homes, or had loved ones to go on to be with the Lord. But God saw fit for you to keep going. Now, as you prepare to cross over to the next season of your life, I am encouraging you to polish your shield. You were created to win this fight! You are well able to go on to do greater things. I am convinced there are men and women reading this book with passions and ideas to impact the world. And because you have stood in your shoes, whatever size they may be, God is rewarding you with continued favor. Doors are already open that you don't even know about yet. So wake up. It's morning! And on this day, the favor of God will lead you on to victory!

21

Deliver Me from Disappointment

We all have a dream down on the inside of us. And each day, we wake up tormented with this same dream. Deep down inside of us there is a force pulling and drawing us towards the possibility that our dreams may come to reality. We wake up thinking: Is today the day? Will that "*something amazing*" happen today? Will I bump into the divine encounter that will change the course of my entire life? We all have a dream.

But when we are expecting God to make our dreams a reality in one specific manner, yet instead we receive a negative report, dissapointment arrives. All sorts of reports come in that tell us things like:

- ❖ Sorry, the door is closed.
- ❖ Sorry, the opportunity is gone.
- ❖ Sorry, we selected somebody else.
- ❖ Sorry, it's too late.
- ❖ Sorry, not this time.
- ❖ Sorry, the disease has spread too far.
- ❖ Sorry, but I give up. This marriage is over and I'm leaving.

It's never easy to get past the hurt of disappointment. It hurts when things just don't work out as you had planned. You feel defeated when you have been working towards something and you find out the project that would have opened so many doors for you has been canceled. The pain of disappointment can be compared to getting pregnant and planning for a baby who is scheduled to come. The nursery is ready, and the clothes are laid out. But then around the 7th month, the doctor tells you, "There is no heartbeat. I'm sorry but the baby is dead in your womb." Disappointment may sometimes mean there is no life left in what you carried, but you are still carrying the dead weight of the dream.

Disappointment hurts even worse when what you were expecting to happen, was due to change your situation from better to worse. When you first get the idea that change is coming, you can seem to put up with the nasty co-workers you don't like a little bit easier. You can deal with not having a home a little bit easier, when you know change is within reach. Riding the bus don't seem so bad when you get the idea that you are about to buy a new car. But when the negative report comes, and you realize you must remain in an already uncomfortable situation longer, the pain of disappointment is hard to avoid.

Esther's Story of Disappointment

> "So they gave Esther's message to Mordecai. Mordecai sent this reply to Esther: 'Don't think for a moment that because you're in the palace you will escape when all other Jews are killed. If you keep quiet at a time like this, deliverance and relief for the Jews will arise from some other place, but you and your relatives will die. Who knows if perhaps you were made queen for just such a time as this?"
>
> (Esther 4:12-16 NKJV)

Esther was raised from a place of poverty, and elevated all the way up to the king's palace as queen, only to find out that her life and the lives of her people are in danger of annihilation.

Jesus' Story of Disappointment

> Then at three o'clock Jesus called out with a loud voice, 'Eloi, Eloi, lema sabachthani?' which means 'My God, my God, why have you abandoned me?'"
>
> (Mark 15:34 NLT)

Jesus spent years healing the sick, raising the dead, and setting people free—only to be led into the most gruesome crucifixion in all of history.

Martha's Story of Disappointment

> "Now Martha, as soon as she heard that Jesus was coming, went and met Him, but Mary was sitting in the house. Now Martha said to Jesus, 'Lord, if You had been here, my brother would not have died. But even now I know that whatever You ask of God, God will give You.' Jesus said to her, 'Your brother will rise again.'"
>
> (John 11:21 NKJV)

Martha waited anxiously for Jesus, knowing that if only her brother could hold out until the healer arrived he would be healed of illness. But Lazarus could not hold on, and Jesus knowingly took his time getting there. As a result Martha's hope for recovery was deferred and her heart became sick with disappointment.

In each of these examples, these staples of hope from bible history were compelled to tap into a force greater than themselves and press beyond the point of disappointment. It serves us no purpose to stand and remain at the crossroad of despair. There is life on the other side of what we think we lost. God may have shut the window of opportunity. But God is also saying get to the door!

There are 10 things we must learn to do in order to recover from our disappointment:

1. <u>Rejoice!</u>

Let's read Paul's inspiration for disappointment:

> "We can rejoice, too, when we run into problems and trials, for we know that they help us develop endurance. And endurance develops strength of

character, and character strengthens our confident hope of salvation. And this hope will not lead to disappointment. For we know how dearly God loves us, because He has given us the Holy Spirit to fill our hearts with His love."

(Romans 5:3-5 NLT)

The moment you find out that things have gone wrong, REJOICE! Rejoice because you are still here. Rejoice because all is not lost. As long as you have breath in your body you have another chance. No matter how the day turns out. This is why we start each day with, "This is the day that the Lord has made, I will REJOICE and be glad in it! And whatever encounters the enemy sends my way, for evil or for my fall, God will ultimately turn it around for my good!"

2. Let God Work

"And we know that God causes everything to work together for the good of those who love God and are called according to his purpose for them."

(Romans 8:28 NLT)

We may not like what we see happening, it may not have been fair—but it's for my good! No matter who left, or what was destroyed. You must believe ultimately it was for your good! It may not *feel* good. But I am a living witness that if you place that encounter and all of the hurt associated with it in the Master's hand; He will work it into His will for your good. Paul Says:

For I am confident of this very thing, that He who began a good work in you will perfect it until the day of Christ Jesus. He who has begun a good work in you shall complete it until the day of Christ Jesus!

(Philippians 1:6 NKJV)

Now you might have a reason to be depressed if you feel like there is nothing going on inside of you. But, you must stop and face your disappointment with an assurance that says, "There is a *great* work going on in me!"

3. Surrender

> And He withdrew from them about a stone's throw, and He knelt down and began to pray, saying, "Father, if You are willing, remove this cup from Me; yet not My will, but Yours be done." Now an angel from heaven appeared to Him, strengthening Him.
>
> (Luke 22:41-43 NIV)

As Jesus prays on the Mount of Olives, he surrenders his will to the Father's will. Then he found the strength he needed to finish the assignment. When it seems that all you have worked for has been futile, it is hard. But you must surrender your will (what you thought should be), for God's will. As you make the decision to surrender, God will dispatch His angels to strengthen you with the confidence and courage to complete the next assignment.

4. Pray

> "Do not be anxious about anything, but in every situation, by prayer and petition, with thanksgiving, present your requests to God. And the peace of God, which transcends all understanding, will guard your hearts and your minds in Christ Jesus."
>
> (Philippians 4:6-7 NIV)

It is very common during your experience of disappointment to become silent. It is understandable that you are at a loss for words. You have prayed all the prayers you know to pray, you have shouted and praised God for the expected victory. And then tragedy happens. You become silent. Lost and confused about how things could have gone wrong, we lose our train of thought. But it is in these times that we must pray more fervently. It is here, at our darkest hour, that we are closest to the light. If we shut up our prayers, we disconnect ourselves from the voice of God which we so desperately need to hear. As bad as it hurts—keep talking to God, keep praying, and keep listening.

5. Be Confident

> "I have written this to you who believe in the name of the Son of God; so that you may know you have eternal life. And we are confident that He hears us whenever we ask for anything that pleases Him. And since we

know He hears us when we make our requests, we also know that He will give us what we ask for."

(1 John 5:13-15 NKJ)

Just knowing that God hears us is winning half the battle. At times we become sorrowful and depressed when we feel as if our situation is hopeless. When we think nobody cares and nobody hears us. But He will never leave us alone nor forsake us. We are never alone. So we can stand strong and be filled with good courage, knowing that our Father hears and sees us. And He will always come see about us!!

6. <u>Fear Not</u>

"Don't be afraid of those who want to kill your body; they cannot touch your soul. Fear only God, who can destroy both soul and body in hell. What is the price of two sparrows—one copper coin? But not a single sparrow can fall to the ground without your Father knowing it. And the very hairs on your head are all numbered. So don't be afraid; you are more valuable to God than a whole flock of sparrows.'"

Matthew 10:28-30 (NKJ)

Many people never attempt to accomplish anything because of the fear of failing. Surprisingly, many times it's the fear of *succeeding* that paralyzes us. But I challenge you to stand up and be courageous! What is there to really fear? Is it the naysayers, haters, or those who wish they could do what you are doing? Or is it simply being afraid of your own success? You may have been told all your life you are worthless. And you may be afraid to prove them wrong. But I dare you to take a stand for yourself! Dare to believe again. Dare to dream like a child again, without a shred of doubt, for the BIG things!

7. <u>Worship—Stay In His Presence</u>

"Nevertheless I am continually with You; You hold me by my right hand. You will guide me with Your counsel, and afterward receive me to glory. Whom have I in heaven but You? And there is none upon earth that I desire besides You. My flesh and my heart fail; But God is the strength of my heart and my portion forever." Psalm 73:23-26 (NKJO)

Don't lean on other artificial vices to get you through disappointment. Artificial vices like excessive eating, excessive drinking, recreational drugs, binge shopping, or anything done in excess to numb you from the pain of your disappointment will fail you. The effects are only temporary. Once the effects wear off you will still be faced with the reality of your current situation.

Don't isolate yourself either. This is when Satan will work in your mind to drag you into a pit of depression. Stay with God, continue to read His word, and keep yourself surrounded by His people. It is in His presence that you will find the courage to forgive. It is in worship that you will find relief through your tears.

During my separation from my husband, I found myself in a very dark and gloomy state of depression. I literally felt like I was buried alive and left to die alone. I vacillated back and forth between blaming myself, to asking God to heal my marriage and my husband's heart and mind, and praying for the strength to let go. The torment of disappointment kept me in a perpetual state of confusion. None of it made sense. Everything about us said we were perfectly joined together by God. But the psychological, verbal, and emotional abuse I endured became too overwhelming. I knew it did not align with what I knew God wanted for my life.

For the first two months after we separated, I was royally devastated. I could not change who my husband or what my marriage had become. And we were inevitably headed for divorce. As we twirled the dance floor at our wedding, I never could have imagined the joy ending. Then during my anguish, I heard God say "Kimberly, hide yourself in Me." I'll admit I didn't start out singing praises and dancing for joy. I came to Him at a loss for words; not able to articulate my pain.

So I started out just crying in His presence. And that's what He wants! Our Father wants us to bring Him our tears. Do you know crying in His presence is still worship? Other times I just sat silently and didn't answer the phone. I didn't want to talk to anyone. I couldn't even listen to gospel music or watch television. Everything was a reminder of my disappointing marriage. But once I really began to open my mouth in worship, the strength to arise began to appear. I found my peace in worship. I found my sanity in worship. I found my roar in worship. I found my joy in worship. It was in consistent worship that God was able to remind me just how valuable I am. It was in worship that I found my 'smile' again. I found the courage to *move on*.

8. Be Humble

"Therefore humble yourselves under the mighty hand of God, that He may exalt you in due time, casting all your care upon Him, for He cares for you"

1 Peter 5:6-7 (NKJV)

Many times when you are disappointed you will want to lash out at someone for your loss. You may want to just go slap off! Ever wanted to give somebody a piece of your mind for causing you to miss a blessing? Somebody must be at fault, and you may really want that person to pay! But regardless of where the fault lies, remain humble. God will get the glory out of your situation. And He will reward you in your humility. But if you put your hand in it, you will miss the blessing.

9. Celebrate

"Fig trees may no longer bloom, or vineyards produce grapes; olive trees may be fruitless, and harvest time a failure; sheep pens may be empty and cattle stalls vacant--but I will still celebrate because the LORD God saves me."

Habakkuk 3:17-18 (CEV)

Celebrate! Not often enough do we celebrate and get excited about the fact that God continues to show up for us. *So what* you haven't gotten the promotion yet! *So what* the spouse hasn't returned yet!

So what you haven't gotten your benefits yet! *So what* you haven't gotten the loan or the car yet! It's easy to fall into a pit of despair when things don't go the way we expect them to. It's frustrating when God does not move on our time table. But no matter what the situation looks like, you have got to find the *celebration* in your *process*. You have got to learn how to dance on your way towards the promise.

You have got to celebrate and give God the praise because you passionately believe His promises are already fulfilled. We are not here but for a moment; a mere blink of God's eye. So I dare you to begin to get up every day and celebrate in a crazy and unexplainable way. I don't care if you are living in a shelter, or if you are depressed in the suburbs. People might think you have lost your mind. But they will soon learn what has happened in your life. It's not that you have finally gotten the tangible reward. But the truth is that you have discovered the secret to how to obtain abundance. You have discovered how to step out of time and walk into eternity. Do you know you don't have to die to experience eternity? You can actaully begin to *live* in eternity by establishing an eternal mindset. That's where real joy is! That's where God is!

10. Trust Him

"The steadfast of mind You will keep in perfect peace, Because he trusts in You."

(1 Peter 5:6-7 NASB)

"Trust in the LORD forever, for in God the Lord, we have an everlasting

Rock." (Isaiah 26:4 NASB)

The tenth and final factor in your deliverance from disappointment is one that receives the greatest recognition: *TRUST IN THE LORD!* As hard as it may be to relinquish control, give the situation to Him. He can see what we can't see. It may not have been fair, it may not look right, but God sees what you can't. So it is because of this very reason that you must release your burdens and your afflictions to Him. The hurt, the pain, and the need for revenge—give it to Him. He's got you covered in ways that you cannot imagine.

When we learn to rest in anticipation of His manifested presence, God gets excited—because then He knows it's His time to shine. It's His time to showcase the beauty of His glory. And *that's* what you were created for: to reflect *His* Glory!

So in hard times and disappointments this is when He gets to arise in us. It is not when things are going smooth and without turbulence that He gets the greatest reward. He doesn't get any glory when you think you are okay to do it alone and without His help. But He gets it in your hurt, in your failures, and in your moments of abandonment and rejection. He gets the glory when your heart has been broken and you have been left for dead. No matter what challenges you face, no matter how devastating the circumstances may appear—you have a place to call home *right in God's heart*. And there you are sure to find peace, love, comfort, and joy in the midst of life's greatest trials. It is when you make yourself at home in His heart that you are sure to find the courage and direction you need to move on. So just kick back, relax and make yourself a cup of tea. Learn how to rest and let God go to work. When you surrender and agree to let Him reign, He will resurrect you from the death that others have eulogized you off to. Get ready to rise, get ready to shine, get ready to dance—because your victory song is just about to begin!

Paid in Full...

Forgiveness is like the bridge that we must all cross to enter the land flowing with milk and honey. Birds are chirping and the sun is shining on the other side. The trees are green and the grass looks soft. The fragrance of the air that blows from the other side smells sweet like honeysuckle. Still, no matter how great things look over there, nobody ever wants to pay the toll to cross.

We show up at the bridge called forgiveness empty-handed and frustrated. We feel as if somebody somewhere has stolen our fare to cross. Somebody raped us, somebody abandoned us, or somebody brutally abused us. And each time, that same somebody took something from us—that piece of our heart that grants us access to live and love freely. When they took something away we entered a deficit. Somebody owes us! *Right?*

Wrong!! The only person that owes you—*is you*. Yes, someone temporarily damaged a piece of your heart. But that can be fixed. Yes, someone ruined precious years of your life. But those can be restored. What they didn't take—couldn't take—was the God in you. And as long as you still have that, they have taken nothing much at all.

If you don't cancel the debts of those who have hurt you, you will wind up charging these debts to the new people that come into your life. And as you do so, you will remain at the bridge wishing each person that passes by would pay the toll for you to cross over into freedom. Do yourself a favor and stop expecting someone else to settle the debts. Nobody wants to pay the price for a crime they haven't committed. God has forgiven them and now you should too. It's time you cross that bridge called forgiveness and cancel the debts of your past. No matter what happened, the blessing is that you are still standing, so they haven't taken anything at all. When you come to the bridge of forgiveness, you will find that the toll for you to cross has already been paid *in full*.

> "And when you stand praying, if you hold anything against anyone, forgive him, so that your Father in heaven may forgive you your sins."
> (Mark 11:25 NIV)

References:

1. Chapter 6 Page 46 "Jesus Saved Us All" www.Wikipedia.com "Emotional intelligence is the capacity of individuals to recognize their own, and other people's emotions, to discriminate between different feelings and label them appropriately, and to use emotional information to guide thinking and behavior."

2. Chapter 7 Page 55 "Confidence to Press Forward" **www.M-W.com** Webster's states that, confidence is, a.) a feeling or consciousness of one's powers, and b.) the quality or state of being certain.

3. Chapter 8 Page 60 "His Workmanship & an Expensive Guarantee" Marvin Sapp- Album: "Here I Am" Released March 16, 2010. Marvin Sapp said it best when he sang, *"He saw the best in me, when everyone else around could only see the worst in ME".*

4. Chapter 12 Page 95 Finding Your place While in the process "TOTAL RECALL" Movie- Released August 3, 2012 by Columbia Pictures

*$_4$**Matthias:** Mr. Hauser, What is it you want?

Doug Quaid: I want to help you.

Matthias: That is not the only reason you are here.

Doug Quaid: I want to remember.

Matthias: Why?

Doug Quaid: So I can be myself, be who I was.

Matthias: It is each man's quest to find out who He truly is, but the answer to that lies in the present, not in the past. As it is for all of us.

Doug Quaid: But the past tells us who we have become.

Matthias: The past is a construct of the mind. It blinds us. It fools us into believing it. But the heart wants to live in the present. Look there. You'll find your answer.

5. Chapter 16 Page 116 "The Enemy, The Soul, & the Promise of Hope" - "Can't Give Up Now" Mary Mary- Album-Thankful Released May 2, 2000

6. Chapter 19 Page 140 "Take it all Back and Then some" **www.m-w.com** - Webster's says that to multiply means "to increase in number by reproducing".

ABOUT THE AUTHOR

Minister Kimberly Michelle Ford, a native of Atlanta Georgia, has committed her life to helping individuals heal and recover from abuse. She is committed to teaching survivors how to maintain a life of freedom as a result of her own personal experience with sexual and domestic abuse. In 2007, Kimberly released her autobiography, "The Core: It's All Inside." In her first book, she ministers to men and women alike who have suffered from the effects of sexual abuse, domestic violence, homelessness, and absentee parents. She recognizes that these are issues that far too many of us have encountered. In 2017, she founded the Freedom Soul Foundation, LLC. to promote Domestic Violence awareness, support, and recovery. The foundation's mission is to enrich the lives of domestic violence survivors and victims' families. Under her leadership, the foundation works to erase the negative stigma associated with speaking out by applauding and rewarding survivors who have exhibited the courage to LIVE. Kimberly Ford is passionate about empowering survivors to live a life of continued freedom from abuse. "Being an advocate for others is not just about helping them to *get free*. Yet, it is also about teaching them how to *stay free*. I pray that as a result of my courage to walk in total freedom, others are inspired to pursue freedom too!"

~Kimberly Michelle

Made in the USA
Columbia, SC
21 September 2017